# CHRISTIANITY AND ISLAM

Published in 1996 by
Marshall Cavendish Corporation
99 White Plains Road
Tarrytown, NY 10591-9001
U.S.A.

*Editor:* Henk Dijkstra
*Executive Editor:* Paulien Retèl
*Revision Editor:* Hans Scheurkogel (The Fall of Rome, The Changing Face of Europe,
The Culture of the Germanic Empires, The New Persian Empire, Muhammad, Islam, Jihad, The Caliphs,
The Riches of Islam), Henk Singor (Constantinople, The Rule of Justinian)
*Art Director:* Henk Oostenrijk, Studio 87, Utrecht, The Netherlands
*Index Editors:* Schuurmans & Jonkers, Leiden, The Netherlands
*Preface:* Abdallah Kahil, Lecturer, Department of Fine Arts, New York University,
New York City

*The History of the Ancient and Medieval World* is a completely revised and updated edition of *The Adventure of Mankind*.
©1996 by Marshall Cavendish Corporation, Tarrytown, New York, and HD Communication Consultants BV,
Hilversum, The Netherlands

Library of Congress Cataloging-in-Publication Data

History of the ancient and medieval world / edited by Henk Dijkstra.
p.  cm.
Completely rev. and updated ed. of: The Adventure of mankind (second edition 1996).
Contents:— v.8. Christianity and Islam.
ISBN 0-7614-0359-0 (v.8).—ISBN 0-7614-0351-5 (lib.bdg.:set)
1. History, Ancient—Juvenile literature. 2. Middle Ages—History—Juvenile literature. I. Dijkstra, Henk. II. Title: Adventure of mankind
D117.H57  1996
930—dc20/95-35715

History of the
Ancient & Medieval World

Volume 8

# Christianity and Islam

*Marshall Cavendish*
*New York  Toronto  Sydney*

# Christianity and Islam

Early Christian sarcophagus decorated with the Good Shepherd and heads of lions

# CONTENTS

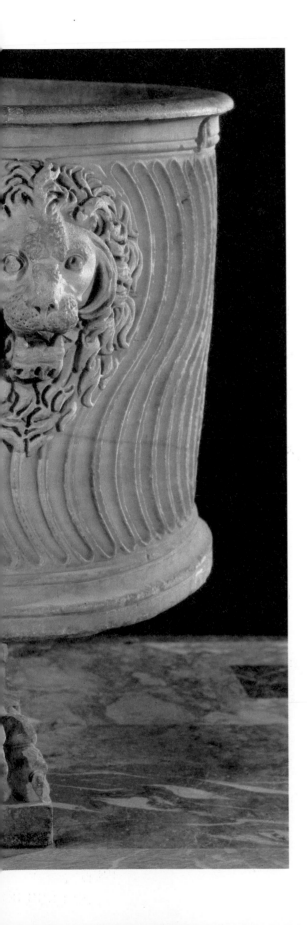

# Preface

The onset of the collapse of the Western Roman Empire in the first quarter of the fourth century AD gave rise to two major monotheistic empires around the Mediterranean basin, the Byzantines and the Muslims. Their expansions were fueled by the political power of their rulers and a common belief in one religion.

When Constantine moved the capital from Rome to Byzantium (later known as Constantinople), Christianity was the official and most predominant religion, and the arts attested to that. Between the fifth and sixth centuries, while the Byzantines ruled most of the eastern part of the Mediterranean and North Africa, their capital was the most splendid city of all. However, the seventh century was a troublesome one for the Byzantines. There was a theological dispute among the clergy, and the borders of the empire became battlegrounds for the powerful Sassanians, who ruled what is now Iraq and Iran, and the Visigoths who ruled from Spain and dominated the western part of North Africa. Even Egypt, which was under the direct dominance of the Byzantine emperor, was disturbed by theological schism.

In the middle of the seventh century, when both Byzantines and their enemies were exhausted, a new power appeared from the most unexpected location: the Arabian Peninsula, proclaiming a religion based on the same political and religious language heard throughout the east. Muhammad, the Muslim prophet, was calling the pagan Arabs to the concepts of the oneness of God and the solidarity of community. He introduced the ideas of equality and peace to warring Arabian factions.

After the death of the prophet Muhammad, the Arabs became relentless in their invasions of western Asia and North Africa; within a century they were at the gates of China in the east and southern France in the west. They decimated the Sassanians, and forced the Byzantines to defend what remained in their hands of Anatolia and the Balkans.

Like all empires, Islam had a heyday as well as a period of fragmentation and decline. Islamic history survived the succession of many dynasties, experienced both unity and schism, and witnessed the interplay of many ethnicities. Throughout this expansive empire the focus shifted from western Arabia to Damascus in Syria, from Baghdad in Iraq to Cairo in Egypt, and from various cities in Persia and Anatolia to cities in Spain.

Meanwhile, new towns were built, many of them highly cosmopolitan. Distinctive styles in architecture and the arts were established, and scientific and philosophical studies based on the achievements of the Greeks, Pahlavis, and Indians were pursued. The predominant language was Arabic, the language of the holy Muslim book, the Koran, though there was an attitude of openness and respect for many of the achievements of ancient and local cultures that the Muslims dominated.

During the middle of the thirteenth century, the Mongol armies arrived from Central Asia, destroying many of the urban centers in Iran and Iraq, including the city of Baghdad, the center of cultural innovations. The fragmentation of the Islamic Empire had begun.

*Abdallah Kahil, Lecturer,*
*Fine Arts Department,*
*New York University,*
*New York City*

Two Roman soldiers guard a prisoner. Detail of the arch of Emperor Constantine in Rome

# The Fall of Rome

## *The End of the Roman Empire*

Although the Roman Empire would ultimately fall to invading barbarians in the fifth century AD, by the third century its structural weaknesses were apparent. A major weakness was the army. It was too small to police the enormous empire internally or to protect it from increasing foreign aggression. Even as the need for more troops grew, Roman interest in military service diminished, forcing increased reliance on foreign recruits from non-Romans on outlying territories. Yet the economic situation made it difficult to fund enough soldiers. Legions concerned with only local defense, and often not fully loyal to Rome, were stationed permanently at the borders, making the army static and incapable of rapid response. Commanders were often under only minimal central authority. The lack of established rules for imperial succession was another weakness. Accession to the throne was often the result of a power struggle involving the family of the emperor, the senate, commoners, and the army. Roman citizenship and the right to vote, once limited to the adult free males of Rome, was granted to all adult freemen living in the Roman Empire by Caracalla in AD 212. (He probably did this in order to levy taxes on the new citizens.) After the death of Alexander Severus, last of the Severan dynasty, in 235, twelve emperors ruled in the next thirty-three years, almost all dying by violence. The emperors of the later third century, notably Claudius II reigning 268–270 and Aurelian reigning 270–275, restored a semblance of peace and unity.

When Emperor Marcus Aurelius Numerianus died in 284, Diocletian (born Gaius Aurelius Valerius, 245–313) was proclaimed emperor by his troops. Ruling between 284 and 305, he introduced a number of reforms that initially benefited the empire but ultimately fostered its decline. Threatened with widespread dissent in the huge empire and wanting to establish orderly succession to the throne, he created a new system of government, choosing his fellow officer, Marcus Aurelius Valerius Maximianus, called Maximian, to share power with him. He titled him *caesar* in 285 and *augustus* in 286.

Diocletian installed two generals under them in rank in 293, titling each one caesar. He adopted one, called Galerius, as his son. Maximian adopted the other, Constantius I. They had the right of succession to the position of augustus. This system, called the tetrarchy, lasted only a year after Diocletian's own resignation. The tetrarchy established separate centers of power in the eastern and western parts of the empire, and set the stage for the eventual division of the empire. Diocletian's other reforms centralized imperial control and ended the traditional primacy accorded Rome.

Diocletian made his capital at Nicomedia in northwestern Asia Minor. Maximian ruled from Mediolanum (modern Milan, Italy). Constantius used Augusta Trevirorum (now Trier, Germany), and Galerius used Sirmium (Sremska Mitrovica, in Serbia). Diocletian abolished the privileges Italy and Rome had been previously given, equalizing them politically and economically with the provinces. He established a government bank and set wage and price controls on food and essentials to regulate inflation. He confiscated land, nationalized mines, and creat-

ed state textile factories. He increased taxes to fund the military and to help the poor. These measures led to an enormous increase in the number of bureaucrats and soldiers and required still higher taxes. To collect them, his government exercised increasing force. His regime was notable, as well, for its persecution of Christians, authorized in 302. In 305, Diocletian and Maximian abdicated in favor of their caesars.

### Constantine the Great (ca. AD 274–337)
The caesar Constantius Chlorus became coemperor as Constantius I. He died within the year. His son Flavius Valerius Constantinus was proclaimed emperor by the troops in 306. Ruling as Constantine, he fought for sole authority until 324.

### Constantine's Conversion to Christianity
Constantine believed in the Roman sun god,

A silver coin,
struck in memory of
the inauguration of
Constantinople

Ivory relief, depicting a personification of the city of Constantinople. The city, also called "New Rome," was founded by Constantine and inaugurated on May 11, AD 330.

Sol, particular protector of Roman emperors. Constantine became embroiled in a four-way conflict with the other caesars and augusti that ended in 312 with his destruction of his Italian rival, Maxentius, at the Battle of the Milvian Bridge, near Rome. According to legend, just prior to the battle, Constantine dreamed that Christ told him to mark the shields of his army with a stylized *XP* (the Greek letters *Chi-Ro*. These were the first letters of the name *Christ*, used as a symbol by the early Christians. The day after he is said to have seen a vision of the cross on the sun, overriding the power of Sol. He said he saw the words *in hoc signo vinces* (Latin for "by this sign you will conquer"). This story was probably told both to gain Christian support and associate a pagan image with a Christian symbol to make Christianity more acceptable.

The church had become popular in the empire despite the efforts of Diocletian to abolish it. The politically astute conqueror Constantine abolished Christian persecution. In 313, with his coemperor, Licinius, who ruled the eastern part of the empire, he proclaimed the Edict of Milan, legalizing Christian worship. His support of the church led to its being given large donations and significant recognition in Europe. He had churches built in Palestine. (His mother Helena, a Christian eventually canonized as St. Helena, is said to have found the cross on which Jesus was crucified.) Although still tolerant of paganism, the emperor presided over the first ecumenical Council of Nicaea in 325. He was baptized shortly before he died on May 22, 337.

### Roma Nova

In 326, Constantine established a new residence and imperial capital at Byzantium, the old Greek colony on the Bosporus. He expanded the little town over the course of

The Battle of the Milvian Bridge, where Constantine beat Maxentius. Detail of a sixteenth-century altarpiece, probably made by Miguel Alcaniz

Detail of a fourth-century fresco on which some crafts and trades are depicted. The fresco was found in Croatia.

six years into a respectable city. Constantine liked to call his creation *Roma Nova*, the New Rome. He had churches and temples built to emphasize the greatness of the empire and adorned the streets with works of art. The new city, renamed Constantinople after its founder, would remain the capital of the Eastern Roman Empire until 1453.

### Government Reforms

In 324, Constantine defeated Licinius, gaining absolute power over the Roman world, east and west. He crowned himself with a pearl diadem as a symbol of his new authority in imitation of the luxurious courts of the east, creating an image of himself as Sol – God on earth. He set about reorganizing

the government under a council, separating civilian and military power, as initiated by Diocletian. At his court, notable for its intrigues, he reformed the senate and created an Order of Imperial Companions, aristocratic, hereditary positions that he governed in authoritarian fashion. Constantine was constantly on guard against conspiracy, and when told by his wife that a son was plotting against him, he had the son (by another wife) killed. Later, thinking it was a terrible mistake, he executed the wife who told him of the plot. Constantine's government was a costly affair. He issued a new standard of exchange, gold coins called *solidi*, to stabilize the currency. His distribution of grain to the poor made him popular with that segment of the population

The two sides of a gold coin with a portrait of Valentinian I, who reigned together with Valens in the period between 364 and 375. The coin was struck in Constantinople.

Aqueduct in Constantinople, built during the reign of Emperor Valens (364–378)

but not with the taxpayers who had to pay the high taxes required to cover his various projects. The economic burden fell heavily on the peasants and landholders, resulting in taxpayer anarchy and corruption among imperial officials.

## Constantius II (?–361)

Constantine's death in 337 led to civil war among Constantine's sons until the middle and only surviving son, Constantius II, seized power in 353. Although he reunited the empire under his rule, he alienated non-Christians by his intolerance and the church by his allegiance to the Arian heresy, which held that Christ was not devine. He appointed his nephew Julian as caesar and made him commander of the Roman army in Gaul.

## Julian the Apostate (ca. 331–363)

Julian (born Flavius Claudius Julianus) campaigned so successfully in Gaul that his troops declared him emperor in 360. When Constantius died in 361, Julian took over Constantinople and Antioch. Called Julian the Apostate for his renunciation of the Christianity he was raised in, he tried to restore the ancient values of old Rome. He proved to be capable although he only ruled for two years. He took steps to minimize the extravagance of his court, diminished the power of the secret police, and introduced stable copper coinage. He was killed fighting the Persians in Mesopotamia on June 26, 363.

## Jovian (ca. 331–364)

The Christian officer Jovian replaced Julian, appointed by the army. Before he died after eight months in office, he attempted to restore the former policies of Constantine.

## The Roman Empire

By the end of the fourth century, three factors combined to bring down the empire. The first was the shift of the center of imperial power from Rome to the east. Second was the growing significance of Christianity, the religion of the state by the turn of the century. Third was the increasing pressure on the borders, especially on the Rhine and the Danube Rivers. With the death of Jovian, the Roman Empire again divided east and west.

## Valentinian I (321–375)

The army replaced Jovian with another Christian officer, the Pannonian Valentinian I, to rule the west. He chose his brother Valens as coregent of the empire in the east. Valentinian I restored Roman authority in Illyricum, Italy, Gaul, North Africa, Spain, and Britain. He was noted for his efforts on the part of the people, especially in the areas of education and medicine.

## Valens (ca. 328–378)

The Goths had left the Roman Empire alone for nearly a century. The two Goth branches, the Visigoths and the Ostrogoths, had founded separate kingdoms in the Ukraine. The situation north of the Danube had stabilized

Remains of an enormous statue of the Roman emperor Constantine, afterward called "the Great." He was the first Roman emperor who converted to Christianity.

The emperor Arcadius, who reigned over the Eastern Roman Empire from 395 on. In practice he left the actual government to his wife Eudoxia and the eunuch Eutropius. He was succeeded by his son Theodosius II in 408.

until the Huns appeared. They seized the Ostrogoth territory and drove the Visigoths toward the Danube.

In 376, the Visigoths sought refuge in the Roman Empire. Valens gladly acquiesced, thinking that they could colonize depopulated land and supply recruits for the army. He offered them parts of Moesia and Thrace, making the Danube River the new border.

In 367, the Visigoths broke the peace. Valens went to war against them. In 378, he was confronted with 20,000 Visigothic warriors outside Adrianople. When the battle was over, Valens and most of his troops lay dead on the battlefield. It was a major turning point in the history of the Roman Empire. The Goths had control of the Balkan

Peninsula. Valens was succeeded as emperor of the east by Theodosius I.

### Gratian (359–383)

In 367, Valentinian I installed his oldest son Gratian as coemperor. A devout Christian, the new emperor rejected the traditional imperial title of *pontifex maximus* (head priest). Although he spent most of his reign battling Germanic invaders in Gaul, he attempted to erase all trace of ancient Roman religion from the empire. After his father's death in 375, he shared rule with his half brother, Valentinian II. His own commander in Britain, Magnus Clemens Maximus, usurped the throne outside of Italy from both in 383, and was proclaimed emperor by Roman troops. Gratian was killed in Lyon that same year.

### Valentinian II (371–392)

The younger son of Valentinian I, Valentinian II acceded to the throne as a minor. His mother functioned as regent until he reached majority in 375. He then shared rule over Italy, northern Africa, and part of Illyricum with his half brother until Gratian's murder in 383. In 387, Magnus Clemens Maximus forced him out of Italy. Valentinian then sought refuge with Theodosius I, whom Gratian had made Roman emperor of the east. Although he briefly recognized Maximus as western emperor in 383, when Maximus invaded Italy in 388, Theodosius I killed him in battle and reinstated Valentinian II. Valentinian II was assassinated in 392, and Eugenius was next on the throne.

### Theodosius the Great (ca. 346–395)

Theodosius defeated Eugenius in September 394. For four months, he was the ruler of both east and west. Born in Spain as Flavius Theodosius, the son of the Roman general Theodosius, he was the last man to rule a unified Roman Empire, if only for four months.

Theodosius I, made eastern emperor by Gratian when Valens was killed in 378, had been crowned the next year. In 382, he had made peace with the Goths, allowing them to live under their own laws and leaders in his empire on condition that they serve in his army. The Goths living in the empire under this arrangement were called *foederati*, or federates. When he died on January 17, 395, the empire was divided between his two sons, Arcadius (ca. 337–408), and Honorius (384–423), neither of them actually suited for the position. The older, Arcadius, was only eighteen and the younger, Honorius, not even twelve years old. Honorius was sent to the west. Arcadius acquitted himself as best he could in the east.

From the third century BC, German tribes wandered through Europe in search of new land. Even the city of Rome was sacked by a tribe called the Vandals. This Roman mosaic depicts a Vandal on horseback. It was discovered during excavations in Carthage.

# The Changing Face of Europe

*Germanic Peoples and Huns Occupy Europe*

The ancient Teutonic people called the Goths had interaction with Romans for centuries before they migrated into the Roman Empire in such vast numbers as to take it over. They were described by Julius Caesar in *Commentaries* in 51 BC and by another Roman, Cornelius Tacitus, in *Germania* in AD 98. The sixth-century Gothic historian Jordanes says the Goths originally came across the Baltic Sea to the Vistula River. The tribes had been in northern Germany and southern Scandinavia since the second century BC when two of them, the Cimbri and the Teutons, invaded Gaul. They had kept the Romans west of the Rhine River in the first century AD.

By the fourth century, joined by other tribes, the Goths under the king Ermanaric had founded a kingdom that ran from the Baltic to the Black Sea. The tribes divided the realm around 370. The Ostrogoths (from the Latin *Ostrogothae* or "eastern Goths") lived east of the Dniester River along the shores of the Black Sea. The Visigoths (from the Latin *Visigothi* or "noble Goths") lived west of them, between the Dniester and the Danube Rivers. These people put increasing pressure on Roman borders until Eastern Roman Emperor Valens let them settle the imperial empire's province of Moesia, south of the Danube, in return for military service. In 378, Valens's Gothic soldiers rebelled against their Roman officers, killing the emperor in battle at Adrianople (Turkey).

Detail of a silver bowl. Theodosius the Great, who was the emperor of the Western Roman Empire in the fourth century, is sitting on his throne in the middle. His sons Arcadius and Honorius, who succeeded him in 395, are sitting next to him.

Twenty thousand Visigoths opposed the Romans. The event foreshadowed the future. By the next century, the Romans were no longer able to defend their borders against the waves of Germanic peoples known as the Great Migrations. Socially organized as tribes, united by language, customs, and eventually by Christianity, they occupied central and western Europe, creating the basis for its modern states. Not only Germany and Austria, but all the English-speaking countries, Scandinavia, Belgium, Switzerland, and the Netherlands speak Germanic-rooted languages today.

Emperor Theodosius I (who succeeded Valens) made peace with the Visigoths,

which stretched from Portugal to the Euphrates and from the Rhine River to the Red Sea. When he died on January 17, 395, the empire was divided between his sons. Arcadius, age eighteen, was sent east to Constantinople where unscrupulous profiteers and plotters took advantage of him. Honorius, not yet twelve, was sent west, where a court official ruled in his name. Theodosius had appointed the Roman general Flavius Stilicho as regent, but slighted Roman dignitaries worked against him. The young emperors were easily manipulated by the powerful men behind the thrones.

## Visigoth Kings
### Alaric I (ca. 370-410)

After the death of Theodosius I, Arcadius, the young emperor in the east, could do little to placate the Visigoths with positions of command and concessions to their leaders. Making Alaric I their king in 395, they sought new territory in the west, migrating in vast numbers. They left their homes and traveled south, encountering little resistance because most of the Roman army was in Italy to support Honorius. They had plenty of time to occupy Illyricum and plunder Greece, sacking Corinth, Argos, and Sparta. Alaric spared Athens in return for ransom. He was subsequently defeated by General Stilicho and forced back to Epirus. There, he managed to gain a commission as Roman prefect of the province of Illyricum from Arcadius, a position he was conceded in a peace agreement. He settled down with his people.

By 401, however, Alaric saw the opportunity to continue expanding his sphere of influence. Gathering up his people, he moved again, this time in the direction of Italy. The Visigoths were already ensconced on the Po Plain when Stilicho heard about the move. In 402, he pulled all the Roman troops out of Gaul and the Rhine border area to stop Alaric. Using all of the empire's reserves, he again succeeded in halting Alaric and the Visigoths at what is today Piemonte, Italy. While Stilicho fought for the kingdom, intrigues at the court of Western Roman emperor Honorius continued unabated. The young emperor eventually convinced Alaric to side with him in an invasion of the Eastern Roman Empire.

With the death of Arcadius in 408, Honorius gave up the idea of invasion. Alaric promptly asked for 4,000 pounds (1,814 kilograms) of gold. Stilicho advised making the payment; Honorius had him executed. He then tossed aside Stilicho's policies, including the agreement that had been made with Alaric. This brought the empire to

Sculptured portrait of Alaric, the king of the Visigoths who conquered Rome at the end of the fourth century. On that occasion, he took the sister of the Roman emperor Honorius as a hostage.

bringing their troops into his army as mercenaries. One of their leaders was Alaric. Their bishop, Ulfilas, translated the Bible into Gothic, enabling large-scale conversions to the Arian form of Christianity (the Son is not of the same substance as the Father but was created as an agent for creating the world).

Theodosius I briefly ruled an empire

Relief on the tomb of the Vandal Stilicho, who was buried in Milan. The relief is in the classical Roman style, but decorative elements typical of northern European art are incorporated in the background.

a new confrontation with Gothic invaders. In Rome, a political party gained power that was opposed to the people it called barbarians, many of whom lived in the empire as *foederati* (federates). The party sponsored a massacre of the families of all the Gothic soldiers in the Roman army. The Goths defected to Alaric.

**The Visigoth Sack of Rome**

The Visigoth king invaded again in 410, besieging Rome and demanding ransom. This time there was no Stilicho to turn him back and he had the newly defected Goths with him. Honorius withdrew to fortified Ravenna. Alaric actually hoped that the emperor would buy him off with supplies and land for his people, but Honorius felt safe in Ravenna. He did not want to negotiate. When all other efforts had failed, Alaric systematically plundered Rome over three

days. Honorius's sister, Galla Placidia, was taken and held hostage by Alaric, but he spared the people. Alaric died while planning to invade Sicily and North Africa.

### Athaulf (?–415)

Alaric was succeeded by his brother, Athaulf, who married Galla Placidia to gain favor with the Romans. He took the Visigoths to Gaul, where a usurper wanted their support as mercenaries. Bought off by Honorius, Athaulf gained significant power in southern Gaul. For the defense of Italy, Stilicho had earlier assembled troops at the Rhine border, giving the Germanic tribes free rein. The Franks set up quarters along the northern borders of the province. The Vandals, the Suebi, and the Alans passed through it without hindrance to conquer areas of Spain. These were formally given to them by Honorius. Various Roman generals, named emperor by their troops, used Gaul as the base for campaigns. One of them drove the Visigoths over the Pyrenees Mountains to Spain, where Athaulf died in 415.

### Wallia (?–418)

Wallia, the next ruler, made peace with the court in Rome. He sent Galla Placidia back and fought successfully for the Romans against the invading Alans and Vandals. Under him, the Visigoths gained control over a great part of Spain and southern Gaul. In 418, the Romans called Wallia back to Aquitania. There, the Visigoths were accorded the status of *foederati* (federates). Assigned places to live, they were permitted self-rule by Honorius in return for military service. Wallia founded the Visigothic dynasty at Toulouse in southwestern Gaul.

As Arian Christians, the Visigoths had a hard time winning the loyalty of their subordinates. Their empire would eventually extend from Lusitania to the Loire, but there were always places where their rule went unacknowledged. The Burgundians had established a foothold in the eastern part of Gaul. Their small empire was a closely knit one, administered by talented kings who had less difficulty with their orthodox citizens than with the Visigoths. From Soissons, the old Roman landowner Syagrius ruled the last part of Gaul, not yet conquered by the Germanics. Although any contact with his superiors in Rome had long been broken, he tried to keep a small piece of the Roman Empire intact.

### Valentinian III (419-455)

The inept Valentinian III succeeded Honorius as Western Roman emperor, installed by the Eastern Roman emperor, Theodosius II. For the early part of his reign, his mother ruled as regent. From 433 on, General Flavius Aetius held power under his nominal authority. They faced Vandals in Africa and Huns along the Danube, in Gaul, and in Italy.

### Theodoric the Great (ca. 454–526)

Theodoric the Great, king after his father's death on the battlefield in 474, founded the Ostrogothic Kingdom in Italy. Held hostage as a child by the Byzantine Empire in Constantinople, he eventually allied with the Byzantine emperor Zeno. In 488, he invaded Italy and defeated Odoacer, its first Germanic ruler. Blockading Odoacer in Ravenna (Italy), he forced him to surrender and then killed him in 493. Theodoric then declared himself the new king of Italy.

### The Huns

The Asian nomads called the Huns had arrived in the Danubian provinces from Mongolia and the Caspian steppes over the course of the fourth century. They may have been related to a tribe from western China called the Hsiung-nu, which had divided over the second century. The Huns were a factor (along with famine) in the Germanic migration west, displacing the Goths as they entered their homeland. The Hsiung-nu people had migrated west to the Caspian steppes and northwest to the Volga River.

In the fourth century, they had fought the Germanic Alans who lived between the

Roman coin dating back from the beginning of the fifth century. Galla Placidia is depicted on the front. She was the sister of Emperor Honorius.

Volga and the Don Rivers. About 375, they had set the Ostrogoths' migration west to the Danube River. The Visigoths fled them for the protection of the Roman Empire. The Huns kept coming, raiding the Eastern Roman Empire on their small, swift steppe horses. By AD 432, under their king Roas (or Rugilas), they were paid annual tribute by Roman Emperor Theodosius I. Noted for their military skill and their mobility, the Huns lived on their horses. (It was said that warriors put raw meat under their saddles to tenderize it and ate as they rode. No one had heard of their losing a fight.)

The Hunnish Empire, by the time of Roas's death, extended from the Rhine River east to the Ural River. It ran from the Danube River north to the Baltic Sea.

### Attila (ca. 406-453)

Roas's nephews Attila and Bleda succeeded him. Attila, who styled himself "the scourge of God," murdered his brother Bleda in 445. Two years later, he conquered the area between the Black and the Mediterranean Seas, forcing the male inhabitants into his army. Riding on to Constantinople, Attila's horsemen turned out to have no way to besiege the city. The Huns contented themselves with tribute from the Byzantine emperor Theodosius II and the lands he gave them south of the Danube.

In 451, Attila led a wide-scale invasion of Gaul in alliance with the Vandals and their king, Gaiseric. At two places, near Koblenz and Basel, his troops crossed the Rhine. Subordinate Gepides, Alans, and Ostrogoths sent large contingents to join the Hun assault. There was no resistance. The Franks, who occupied the banks of the Rhine in the north, let the army pass unchallenged.

The Roman general and *de facto* (in fact) emperor Flavius Aetius was in southern Gaul with an army. As soon as he heard of the invasion, he sought reinforcements, aware that he could not defeat the Huns alone. He convinced the Visigoths, fellow Christians, and Roman foederati to join him. The allied forces traveled north toward Attila's army. They met the Huns in the Catalaunian Plains at Châlons-sur-Marne in 451.

Attila, the legend says, summoned his soothsayers to foretell the outcome of the battle. Scorching the *scapulae* (shoulder blades) of sheep and tortoise shells, they read from the cracks in them that Attila would be defeated but that his enemy would die.

The battle was a bloodbath. Contemporary historians estimated Attila's losses at over 200,000 killed (now believed exaggerated). The Huns had allied with the Gepides, the Herules, and the Ostrogoths against the Roman legions, the Visigoths, and a few Franks. Attila shot the first arrow, fighting throughout the battle in the front lines. Theodoric I, who had reigned as king of the Visigoths since 419, was also in the forward line. Wounded by a Hun spear, he died.

Leaf of an ivory *diptych* (having two leaves or panels) with the portrait of the Roman general Stilicho, who lived at the end of the fourth century

A soldier from the infantry of the Visigothic army, depicted in a manuscript from the year 1109

Seal of Alaric II, with the text *Alaricus rex Gothorum* written in reverse. Alaric was defeated by Clovis in 507.

Attila's enemy (but not Aetius) had fallen, as predicted. Toward evening, Roman charges forced the Huns to retreat, with the Visigoths in close pursuit. Then Aetius, to their amazement, asked the Goths to cease their attacks. They withdrew to Toulouse, allowing Attila to leave Gaul unhindered.

Attila recovered quickly, moving down the Alps to the Po Plain of Italy the following year. He began a march toward Rome. Milan, Pavia, Aquileia, and other cities of northern Italy paid tribute to avoid conquest. Some of their inhabitants fled his advance to the delta marshes of the Po and the Piave Rivers near the northern end of the Adriatic Sea. The region was inhabited by the Veneti people. In 452, the refugees founded the city of Venice on the many islands there. It would grow into the largely independent republic of Venice, nominally part of the Eastern Roman Empire.

Rome sent emissaries to intercede with

Roman sarcophagus from the fourth century depicting a battle between Romans and barbarians

Attila. Among the mediators was Pope Leo I. Exactly what took place in the tent of the generals is uncertain, but after the conference, Attila withdrew. "Attila, thou art the most mighty conqueror," Pope Leo is said to have told him, "Thou hast conquered thyself." Attila died in 453.

### The Roman Empire Becomes a Germanic Kingdom

Aetius only outlived his dreaded opponent for a few months. He was murdered in 454 by the young emperor Valentinian III. Two years later, Valentinian was murdered by friends of Aetius in retaliation.

Over the twenty years following the death of Valentinian III in 456, nine Roman emperors would rule in succession. The man behind the throne was the Suebe general Ricimer (he died in 472). The leader of the Germanic contingent in the Roman army, the Herulian Odoacer (who lived from about 433 to 493), overthrew the last emperor of Western Rome, Romulus Augustulus, in 476. His soldiers, demanding the same rights as the other foederati over recent years, declared him king. He sent the insignia of the Western Roman emperor to Constantinople, demanding and getting recognition of his authority. The Western Roman Empire had become a Germanic kingdom.

The Heruli people Odoacer came from were Teutonic, originally from Scandinavia. With the Goths, they had been raiding the coasts of the Black and Aegean Seas since the third century. By the sixth century, they would establish their own Heruli Kingdom in the Elbe River basin, only to see it destroyed by the Lombards.

Meanwhile, around 480, a period of stability ensued under Odoacer. He ruled in reasonable cooperation with the Roman Senate as the first Germanic king of Italy. In 493, he would surrender to and be killed by the Ostrogothic king Theodoric the Great, son of the king slain by the Huns at Châlons-sur-Marne in 451.

### The Vandals

The Vandals were among the earliest Germanic peoples to migrate to the Danube River region. Originally from Jutland, now part of Denmark, they had settled along that river over the second and third centuries, moving to the Oder River valley in the fifth century. Under Godigiselus, they first entered Gaul in 406. Gunderic succeeded Godigiselus that year and led the Vandals on to Spain three years later. They had already founded a new kingdom there when the Visigoths fell upon them under orders from Roman authorities. The Visigoths annihilated the Vandal population in such numbers that the Romans were shocked and offered the Vandals land in Aquitania. Now left alone by the Visigoths, Gunderic and the Vandals took on the Suevis who occupied, with Rome's blessing, the south of Spain. He was replaced by his brother Gaiseric (or Genseric) in 428.

## Gaiseric (ca. 400-477)

The natural son of Godigiselus, King Gaiseric led the tribe out of Spain across the Straits of Gibraltar to North Africa the following year. The Vandals found it quite easy to conquer the countryside. They forced the Roman general Bonifacius out of Africa to Italy. By 435, they had seized most of the western Mediterranean coast. With their primitive fighting tactics, however, the Vandals could not readily take over the major cities. Not until 439, ten years after their arrival, were the Vandals able to capture Carthage. Gaiseric used the city as his capital. His sovereignty and the independence of the Vandal Kingdom were recognized by the Western Roman emperor Valentinian III in 440.

The new rulers of Africa proved to be talented seamen. Their fleets drove the Romans from the Mediterranean, which they had called *Mare Nostrum* (our sea) for five centuries. The Vandals plundered the islands of Sardinia, Corsica, and Sicily. Gaiseric was even able to take the Sicilian fleet base of Lylibaeum.

## The Vandal Plundering of Rome

In 455, the emperor Valentinian III died. The Vandal king used the death as rationale to invade Rome. This time the negotiating talents of Pope Leo I were unable to prevent the sacking, although Gaiseric agreed to spare civilian lives. The Vandals entered the city unopposed. They plundered it for fourteen days, carrying away as much as they could of

value, including the last vestiges of the city's prestige. (This extensive looting of Rome gives the word *vandal* its household connotation today.) Gaiseric took Eudoxia, Valentinian's widow, and her two daughters as hostages and a great many Roman citizens as slaves.

Illustration from a medieval manuscript. Clovis, the leader of the Franks who converted to Christianity, is here baptized by two bishops. The Holy Spirit, depicted as a dove, brings a little can of oil.

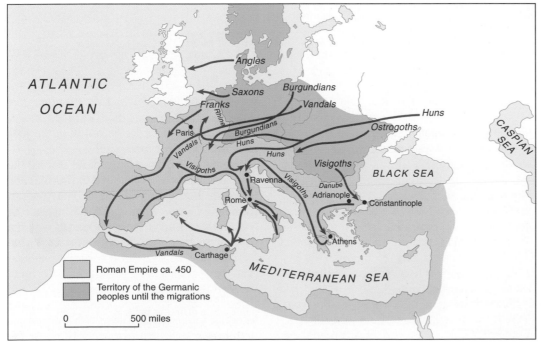

Invasions of hostile peoples in the Western Roman Empire during the fourth and fifth centuries

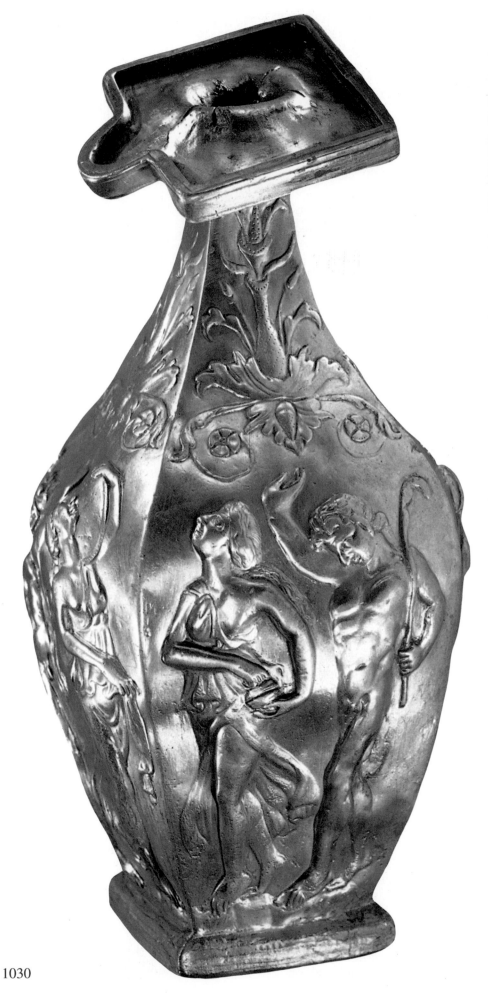

### The Vandals Go East

The triumphant Gaiseric went on toward the east, headed for Constantinople. En route, he pillaged Greece and Dalmatia. The Western Roman emperor Majorian tried unsuccessfully to stop him in 457. Marjorian was the first of several emperors put in place by the

Silver vase
from the fifth century
depicting a drinking bout.
The vase was discovered
in Romania.

Suebe Ricimer (called the kingmaker in Rome); he reigned from 457 to 461.

The Eastern Roman emperor Leo I tried again in 468, with equal lack of success. The Vandals were Arian Christian, opposed theologically to the Eastern Orthodox Christians of Leo's Byzantine Empire. Finally, in 476, the Eastern emperor Zeno recognized Gaiseric's authority and made peace with the Vandals. Gaiseric died the next year and their power began to disintegrate. Under the surface, there were forces at work which would make them easy prey for the Eastern Roman armies.

Gaiseric was succeeded by his son Hunneric, who reigned from 477 to 484. At their peak, the Vandals controlled the former Roman provinces of Africa, Mauritania, Sardinia, Corsica, and the Baleares. Under Hunneric, Vandal power, especially in Africa, continued its decline. In 534, the Vandals were finally brought down by the Byzantine general Belsarius.

## The Franks
The Germanic people called the Franks had established themselves along the Rhine

Pope Leo the Great meets Atilla the Hun, who is heading for Rome with his army. The pope succeeded in dissuading Atilla from sacking the city. This fresco, in the papal quarters of the Vatican, was made by the Renaissance artist Raphael in the sixteenth century.

Painting of Atilla
the Hun, who was nicknamed
"the scourge of God"

center of power had evolved in Tournal, ruled by a king named Childeric I. Little more is known about him other than the fact that he died in 481. His fifteen-year-old son Chlodowech succeeded him. Known to history as Clovis I, he was the first important ruler of the Merovingian dynasty. The young king expanded the kingdom through conquest, treachery, murder, and war. In 486, he marched on the city of Soissons, northeast of Paris, seizing the holdings of the Roman Empire in Gaul from its governor Syagrius. He continued his conquests in that region for several years.

In 493, Clovis married Clotilda, the Christian daughter of Chilperic, king of Burgundy. In 496, he destroyed the army of the Alemanni, who had established a federation of Germanic tribes along the upper course of the Rhine to the east. According to legend, he called upon his wife's god at a critical moment in the battle. His victory and undoubtedly the influence of Clotilda led to Clovis's conversion to orthodox Christianity later that year. (Born about 470, Clotilda joined a convent at Tours after her husband died, until her own death in 545. She was canonized, called a saint by the church, a few years later.)

In 496, the king was baptized in Reims, together with most of the important people of his court. The baptism made Clovis and his Franks (a group familiar to the Gauls and close to them in customs) popular far beyond the reaches of his kingdom, particularly among the clerical elite. Already the most powerful figure in the north, his conversion to Christianity was an excellent idea politically, winning him the loyalty of his subjects and laying the basis for a close-knit empire. It also enabled him to position himself as religious liberator in all further wars that he fought, gaining the support of the church as he campaigned.

By 506, he had subdued the Alemanni. In 507, he killed the Visigoth king Alaric II in battle near Poitiers. He had pushed the Visigoths back over the Pyrenees. Only Septimania, the coastal strip between Spain and the Rhone, remained in Gothic hands. Clovis made Paris his capital. When he died in 511, he was the undisputed ruler of a Frankish kingdom that stretched from the Rhine to the Pyrenees and from the Main River to the Atlantic Ocean. It was divided among his four sons.

River over the third century AD. The tribe was divided into two main groups, the Ripuarian Franks, who inhabited the middle section of the river, and the Salian Franks, on its lower reaches. The Salians were conquered in 358 by the Roman emperor Julian. They were subsequently accepted in the Roman army as foederati. In 402, the Roman general Stilicho withdrew his troops from the Rhine to stop Alaric's invasion of Italy. The Salians took over the region. At the underdeveloped periphery of the old empire, they led a traditional Germanic life, only minimally touched by cultural influences from the south. They worshiped gods of the sun and thunder, Wodan and Freya.

### Clovis I (ca. 466-511), King of the Franks (481-511)

By the fifth century, a small Salian Frankish

The Germanic god Odin rides through the world on his eight-legged horse, Sleipnir. His ravens, who gather news for him, are flying over his head.

# The Culture of the Germanic Peoples

## The Franks, Ostrogoths, Visigoths, and Lombards

Although the precise time when the Middle Ages began cannot be ascertained, some historians have placed it at the moment in 476 when the Herulian Odoacer's cheering soldiers lifted their leader upon his shield. He had just deposed Romulus Augustulus, the last Roman emperor. Roman authority had been rendered subordinate to the Germanic. The Gothic king was recognized by the Eastern emperor Theodosius II in Constantinople.

Although the political change was significant, Europe in the Middle Ages was still heir to the legacy of classical Rome. It was also profoundly influenced by the Great Migrations of Germanic peoples that took place over the second to the fifth centuries. This was less a matter of numbers than of might. There were not enough invaders to drive out the indigenous residents. In 378, it was at most 20,000 Visigoths who battled

Emperor Valens and his Romans at Adrianople. The Lombards, who entered Italy in the sixth century, numbered a mere 200,000, women and children included. All the Germanic tribes could do was to estab-

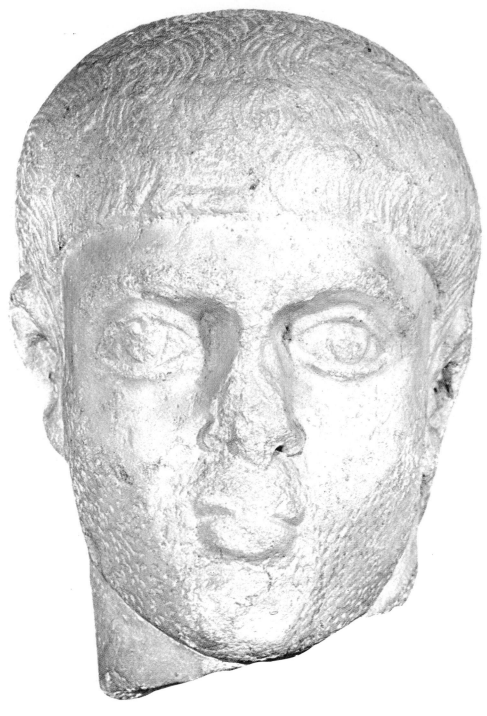

Portrait of the Western Roman emperor Avitus (455–456), who was deposed by the Visigothic leader Ricimer

lish themselves among the original inhabitants and take control of their government. Germanic conquest was due more to Roman weakness than Gothic strength. For centuries, the legions of Rome had been able to fight off foreign invaders. Now the exhausted empire could no longer cover the expenses of its own upkeep. It employed foreigners in those legions, pitting them against each other as it fought for its own survival. The foreigners did not consider it shameful to

serve the mighty empire. They took the view that if the empire wanted to utilize a foederati, it was merely evidence of the Goths' ability. Clovis I, the Frankish king who united the Riparian and Salian Franks and created the Merovingian dynasty, was said to have been flattered when he received a badge of honor from the Byzantine consulate. Theodoric, who conquered Odoacer and established the Ostrogothic Kingdom of Italy, requested the East Roman emperor for permission to wear the royal crown.

Roman civilization made an overwhelming impression on the invaders. Even though the actual power of the Western Roman emperor was eventually limited to Italy, he continued to have considerable prestige. This carried over to the east and the emperor in Constantinople after the deposition of the last western emperor. Although their own cultures were ancient, the Germanics were not at all technically advanced. They marveled at Rome's temples, the now-depopulated *insulae* (public apartment houses), and the caved-in aqueducts built by earlier generations. Limited in their own academic knowledge, they observed Roman art, science, and literature and tried to learn from it. Germanic leaders saw the Roman high officials in all the trappings of office and attempted to imitate them, and coveted positions of honor. They collected treasures made by Roman hands.

**The Hospitium**

In order to obtain places to live, the Germanic tribes made use of an old Roman custom, the *hospitium* (visitor's rights). Although this carried an obligation on the part of the recipient of the hospitality, it eventually became a euphemism for billeting soldiers. Indigenous landowners had to provide housing for foreign invaders. The new inhabitants usually complied with regulations. They had an interest in living close together for military reasons. They did not want to be dispersed throughout the Roman areas they controlled. In other senses, as well, the invaders behaved like guests. They did not concern themselves with the lifestyles and customs of those they conquered. The Germanic tribes did not try to change the law, the distribution of wealth, or the official hierarchy of areas they conquered. Living among the original inhabitants, they led their own lives according to their own traditions, brought with them across the Rhine and Danube Rivers. These otherwise parallel lines of custom converged only at the king. He held supervisory authority over the entire government. The Burgundian king Gundobad issued two sep-

Merovingian *sarcophagus* (stone coffin) in the crypt of St. Seurin (Bordeaux)

arate law books, the *Law of the Burgundians* and the *Roman Law of the Burgundians*.

Little altered for the masses of the Roman people. They had a new elite class at the top and a rarely seen royal tax collector. The farmers of North Africa were said to prefer the new Vandal administrators to their former rulers from Rome. There was, however, a problem of religious difference. Most new rulers held beliefs different from those of their subjects, creating problems of popular loyalty. While Romans elsewhere left their subjects alone in terms of their beliefs, the Vandals frequently persecuted those who disagreed with them.

## Arianism

The Goths, if Christian at all, subscribed to its Arian form of belief, largely because of the Christians who converted them were Arians. Most notable among them was Ulfilas, the Christian bishop who translated the Bible into Gothic. Arianism, banned in 379 as heresy in Rome, existed among the Goths at least another two centuries. Named for Arius, the fourth-century Libyan theologian who was its greatest proponent, it concerned the divinity of Jesus Christ. Although Arius was exiled in 325 to Illyria, his views continued to spread.

His point was that only God is "unbegotten" or uncreated. Traditional Christians took the view that God, Jesus, and the Holy Spirit (Father, Son, and Holy Ghost; the Trinity) were all of the same divine essence.

Condemned in the west, Arius was reinstated in the east by Emperor Constantine I in 334 and supported by Emperor Constantius II. Eusebius of Nicomedia, patriarch (head of the Orthodox Church) of Constantinople was an Arian. By 359, Arian Christianity was made the state religion.

1035

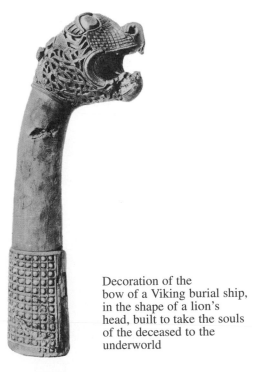

Decoration of the
bow of a Viking burial ship,
in the shape of a lion's
head, built to take the souls
of the deceased to the
underworld

< The god Wodan
rides his horse in the air.
This drawing was made by
Arthur Rackham
for an edition of *Der Ring der
Nibelungen*, ancient
Germanic legends of gods
and heroes.

Arian advocate Constantius II died in 361, succeeded by the anti-Arian emperor Valens. The next emperor, Theodosius, accepted the Nicene Creed in 379. Its principles, condemning Arianism, were adopted by the second ecumenical council held in 381.

It was only in the course of the sixth century that the religious chasm was bridged. The Burgundians and the Visigoths switched to the orthodox beliefs, but this no longer had much political effect.

### The Organization of Power

By the end of the fifth century, although many Goths had received status as foederati, serving as soldiers to defend the empire in return for land or other concessions, they knew that real power lay with their own leaders. Many Goths formally carried out administrative tasks in the name of Roman authority, but both the emperors and the tribal heads knew that Roman central authority was at an end.

The political structure that the Germanic conquerors brought with them underwent major changes as they gained power. The tribes, which once distributed land to their members annually on the basis of social class, suddenly found themselves in possession of vast areas. The Visigoths controlled much of Spain and southern Gaul, the

Detail of a twelfth-century
relief on the porch of
St. Zeno (Verona), depicting
Theoderic and Odoacer
in combat

1037

Lombards held the largest part of Italy, and the Vandals ruled the Mediterranean and the former Roman regions of Africa.

According to *Germania*, written in AD 98 by Cornelius Tacitus, Germanic society of the time was organized around the *pagus* (clan). Many of these clans elected chiefs, limiting their power by tribal council and the *comitium* (groups of men who swore alle-giance to the chief). By the fourth century, clan meetings no longer sufficed as decision-making bodies. Authority shifted from that granted at meetings of all freemen to a single king. The nature of the empire itself demand-ed a monarchic system, although the concept of a royal dynasty was virtually unknown. The king was chosen by the members of his bloodline. His most important function was

Germanic talisman in the shape of a hammer. This was the symbol of the god Thor, who could strike lightning with his hammer.

1038

Sixth-century helmet, found in a burial chamber in Krefeld, Germany

# The Fate of the Britons

During the third century, the Roman province of Britannia was not a major concern of the Roman Empire. Rome itself was threatened and people in other parts of the empire were busy coping with roaming bands of plunderers. Beginning in 400, the Frisians, the Jutes, and the Anglo-Saxons traveled from Scandinavia in their simple, efficient ships to plunder the British coasts. When the Visigoths invaded Rome in 410, the Roman garrison was withdrawn from Britannia to assist in its defense. In the north of Britannia, Picts and Scots raided the countryside. They breached the Antonine Wall across the narrowest part of the island and also, twenty miles (32 kilometers) south of it, Hadrian's Wall, both built by the Romans some two hundred years earlier. The Britons sent a final cry for help to Rome, to no avail. Rome had abandoned the province. Celtic culture, brought by migrants to Britannia centuries earlier, again predominated as Roman influence diminished.

The Angles and Saxons invaded Britain in the fifth and sixth centuries. Many Britons, remembering their Roman past, fled across the English Channel to the Roman province called Armorica. Located in northwestern France, the region would eventually be called Brittany after these Britons (later, Bretons) who kept their own language and customs.

It took the Angles and Saxons more than a century to establish a predominant culture on the islands. About AD 500, they were defeated in a battle linked to the name of Artorius. He was the historical figure on whom the legends of King Arthur and his knights of the Round Table were based. Artorius is believed to have traveled the land with a division of soldiers that had been trained by the Romans, protecting his countrymen wherever he could.

Miniature from the twelfth century, depicting knights fighting each other on horseback

---

serving as commander in chief of the army. Those who performed well here, like Alaric and Theodoric, rose to great power. The new subjects, primarily Roman citizens, were accustomed to responding to a single powerful leader and readily adapted to following the new conquerors.

Tribal kings began to rule from set places of residence, following the model of the Roman court. Each king assembled a group of officials around his throne to take care of imperial administration. Each also appointed a *major domus* (mayor of the palace) to manage the royal household. This official eventually acquired greater influence than the ministers and the judges appointed by the

Roman Empire. The members of the former Roman elite usually cooperated with the new rulers, but did so out of recognition of political reality. Only in instances where the new king was an orthodox Christian could he count on the loyalty of his subjects.

## Germanic Laws

Once the Teutonic empires were established on Roman soil, their kings, again following the Roman pattern, attempted to record their traditional laws in writing. None of the codes was extensive. The recording of actual cases so as to provide a body of legal precedent was virtually unknown.

Penal law was notable in two respects:

Fresco depicting
the court of Autari, who was
a Longobard leader at
the end of the sixth century.
This picture was made
much later, and is a part of
the altar in the cathedral
of Monza.

almost all crimes were punishable by fines and divine judgment was invoked on a large scale. It was assumed that God would allow injury only to the guilty. Trial by fire was common. Suspected criminals had to grip a red hot poker,  walk barefoot over burning coals, or reach into boiling water to retrieve a stone. Those who healed were presumed innocent, whereas if they became infected, they were pronounced guilty.

Sometimes the accuser rather than the suspect had to undergo trials by ordeal. If a Lombard accused a woman of being a witch or a prostitute, he had to prove himself in a *kampfio* (ritual fight). The law specified that participants in such fights could not be protected by magic spells.

Punishment meant, in nearly all cases, a fine. The Germanic tribes had a concept of defense money, assigning every person (and even several animals) a specific value. That amount was higher in proportion to rank. If a person harmed or killed another person, he had to pay the calculated defense money to the relevant party. A blow that fractured the skull and exposed the brain cost thirty solidi, under Frankish law. Under Lombard law, "for blows to the head which cause a fracture of the base of the skull, one must pay twelve solidi for each bone." Putting out a person's eye or chopping off a nose was fined by six solidi.

Each front tooth was worth seventeen solidi; each molar half of that. Killing a pregnant woman was fined by four times the defense money of a freeman. An abortion cost a hundred solidi. The Lombard legislator explained: "For all of these injuries and fights which can occur between freemen, we have arranged settlements which are more liberal than those our ancestors applied, so there will

Miniature from the *Liber Iudicorum* (*The Book of Judges*), an early medieval code of law that was made by order of a Visigothic leader

1041

come an end to the *faida* (feud) or disagreement, and so that one will bear no grudges, but instead that those who had been enemies can live as friends. Defense money differed from group to group. Insults, too, were punishable. There were specified fines for calling someone names, for example: "fox," "hare," "spy," or "liar." "Sly fox" and "hare" cost three denarii each; "liar" cost fifteen.

Most specifications concerning physical

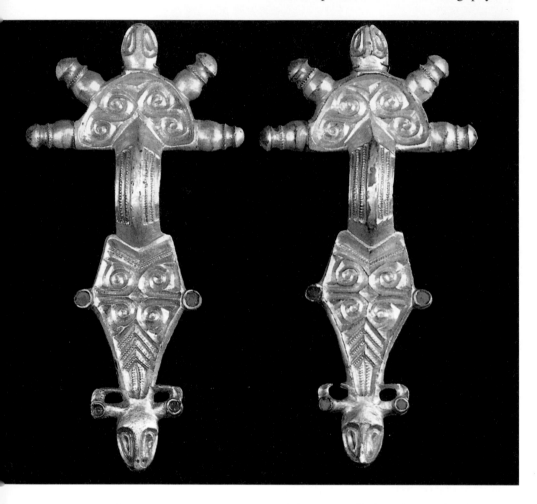

Two *fibulae* (cloak pins), made by the Visigoths

punishment applied to slaves. If a slave stole something small, the law sentenced him to 120 blows, because he owned no property. If he stole more, he was castrated. The principle behind these laws was reimbursement to the victims of crime. This differed from that of the Romans, whose goal was punishment of criminals. The Germanic fines were intended as compensation to the victims rather than as punishment. Roman law was not entirely lost during this time. A rudimentary version of it still applied to the vanquished population. Roman jurisprudence would be rediscovered in later centuries.

## Family

Among the seminomadic Germanic tribes, the clan was particularly important. Clan or family obligations were basic to their legal principles. According to Frankish law, any-

one unable to pay his debts could transfer them to his closest relative. He had to swear that he had nothing "upon the earth nor under," then collect a handful of dust from the corners of his hut, throw it on his closest relative, and jump over his fence. He was then declared insolvent. His family would take care of the payment.

There was an established ceremony associated with separating oneself from the family. The individual involved had to appear before witnesses, break four elm branches over his head, and throw them in the four directions. Such secession from the family rendered the usual mechanism of blood revenge inapplicable.

The Germanic concept of family included a man's right of *mundium* (possession) over his wife and other women he had, his children, his slaves, and his freemen. It was quite similar to the Roman concept of possession called *manus*. According to Frankish law, a woman could not inherit land. The law of the Lombards stated, "It is illegal for a free woman to live according to her own will, because she always continues to be subject to the power of a man, husband or relative. Therefore she cannot transfer her property, movable or immovable, without the permission of the person under whose mundium she lives."

Among all Germanic groups, it was customary for the husband to give his wife a "morning gift" on the morning after their wedding night. The wife was expected to give him a dowry, called the *father-tiu* (father's money). The Lombards made careful arrangements for the distribution of property after the dissolution of a marriage, the death of either spouse, or a second marriage. Upon marriage, the wife fell under the mundium of her husband. If he died, his oldest son inherited the mundium. If she had no son, she went back to the mundium of her family. If she had no family, the king appointed a guardian for her, who was obligated to defend her if she were falsely accused. Illegitimate children had a legal right to at least a small portion of inheritance. Disinheriting children was not permitted. The property of anyone who died childless became the property of the king. Some people who had no successors would give away their land while they were still alive in order to prevent that.

A man suspected of having killed his wife had to swear a *sacramentum* (an oath) that he was innocent in the presence of witnesses. In less serious crimes, the suspect had to take an oath of innocence on his weapons. The case would continue after the oath until agreement on a verdict was reached.

As contact between the inhabitants of the Roman Empire and the Goths increased, so did intercultural communication and intermarriage. This had an eventual effect on language.

## Germanic Languages

The Goths left a legacy of Indo-European Germanic languages used today by almost 500 million people not only in Europe, but wherever Europeans colonized. Gothic language itself (or East Germanic), including Vandal, is extinct.

The North Germanic or Scandinavian language group is used in Icelandic, Norwegian, Fareoese (an Icelandic-Norwegian dialect), Danish, and Swedish. West Germanic is the basis of the Netherlandic and Dutch-Flemish languages, High and Low German, Afrikaans (spoken in South Africa), and Yiddish. The Anglo-Frisian branch of West Germanic includes the minor Frisian language of the North Sea region and, in far greater use, the English language.

During the existence of the Roman Empire, Latin had dominated the local languages. In the early Middle Ages, it continued to be the only official language in most of western Europe. All deeds, laws, and decrees were written in it. These texts were badly written, full of spelling and grammatical errors, but they laid the basis for the Romance languages of present-day Europe. Local people adapted Latin to their own use, evolving regional dialects which grew further apart over the centuries, particularly where contacts between former Roman provinces decreased.

The basilica of Palencia (Spain), dedicated to John the Baptist. This church was built by the Visigoths in the seventh century.

Gold plate with a picture of a Longobard soldier

## Cultural Decline

Under the Goths, the former Roman Empire continued the economic and cultural decline that had already begun before their takeover. The Germanic rulers had little interest in economic development or trade. To them, the only thing that mattered was land. They formed nations composed of farmers who produced enough to supply the needs of the people living on their land.

Local communities were expected to be self-sufficient; trade existed only in a limited way. Merchants were vendors who brought back luxurious articles from faraway places, making trade a fringe element within the all-encompassing agricultural economy. The circulation of money virtually ceased. The kings occasionally had a few gold coins minted, but these had a very high value and were seldom taken out of the treasury. Europe returned to an agrarian society.

Most Roman cities disintegrated. The great empire-wide organization of engineering projects stopped. Little construction went on, even for repairs. Small service areas continued to exist only around the residences of bishops and noblemen. In Rome itself, the ancient monuments were demolished for their stone and the forum became a meadow. Temple pillars were used in building churches. The aqueducts collapsed, the resulting floods turning the region outside Rome into swampland.

Cultural knowledge from Roman times was lost everywhere except the monasteries. Latin became a written instead of a spoken language, learned only by the elite and read by monks. Most people spoke another language and were illiterate. Latin was restricted to church services, reserved for God and the powerful. Even the Germanic kings had never learned to read and write, leaving such intellectual matters entirely to their priests. Laymen were concerned with agriculture and battle.

As the Western Roman Empire was taken over by the Goths, an eastern or Byzantine emperor still reigned at Constantinople. The successors of Arcadius had managed to drive out the enemies of their empire. At the end of the fifth century, the throne was reasonably secure. Soldiers were recruited from the indigenous population, the bureaucracy functioned, and the rule of the emperors remained largely uncontested. Those rulers in the east had never lost their interest in the west. Still hoping to win back their lost territories, clever diplomats played the Germanic kings against each other, bribing them as necessary. By the sixth century, the east was gathering force to reconquer the west.

The two sides
of a Visigothic coin,
a *tremis* (one-third
of a *denarius*)

Miniature from
the Codex Albendensis,
depicting an unknown
Visigothic ruler

1044

These four bronze horses once decorated the Hippodrome (racetrack) of Constantinople. After the sack of the city by the Crusaders in 1402, they were taken to Venice and placed over the entrance to the basilica of San Marco.

# Constantinople

*A New Capital in an Old City*

In 324, the Western Roman emperor Constantine defeated his eastern Roman counterpart, Emperor Licinius (ca. AD 270–325). He decided to establish his new residence and capital at the old Greek colony of Byzantium. Famous throughout antiquity for its favorable location, it lay on the narrow Strait of Bosporus, between the Black and the Mediterranean Seas. The strait separates the continents of Europe and Asia.

Byzantium had been recognized as a free confederate city by the Romans in 65 BC in return for Byzantine help in earlier wars. Its citizens were asked to pay tribute to Rome

1045

during the reign of Emperor Claudius I (AD 41–54). In 194, the Byzantines supported Pescennius Niger against the Roman emperor Lucius Septimius Severus. When Severus captured the city in 196, he demolished its walls and ended its privileged status.

By the time Constantine took over in 324, Byzantium was poor, its citizens down-trodden. Once Constantine had decided to establish his new residence there, however, Byzantium experienced dizzying growth. Ambitious architects began to transform the miserly Byzantine street layout into a residence worthy of the emperor. An army of workmen labored on the *Mesè*, a boulevard without equal in the *oikoumenè* (ecumenical district). Above the massive blocks of housing, the domes of the churches soon reached toward the sky. Seamen could see the emperor's bronze palace glittering in the sun from far away.

Constantine made the city a home for the Christian elite of his empire. His wide-scale distribution of grain to the poor attracted innumerable immigrants. His fleets brought in art treasures from all over the empire.

On May 11, 330, the city was officially dedicated as the new capital, an event that would continue to be celebrated each year on that date. The city was referred to as *Nova Roma* (New Rome) to indicate its primacy over Rome. Constantine renamed it Constantinople after himself. People streamed in from all over the empire, raising the population to several hundred thousand residents.

Constantine could not have established his headquarters at a better place. Constantinople lay on a peninsula between the Sea of Marmara, which emptied into the Black Sea on the north, and the Golden Horn, a narrow inlet of the Bosporus. This reached over six miles (9.6 kilometers) inland, providing ready access to the sea and its shipping routes. From the huge palaces on the Bosporus, the city ribboned over seven hills to the massive walls that enclosed the peninsula. The city ramparts ran from the Golden Horn to the Sea of Marmara, some two and a half miles (4 kilometers) from ancient Byzantium.

The growth of the city over the fourth and fifth centuries, as well as its consequent interest in security, inspired Emperor Theodosius II to construct new walls a few miles (five kilometers) outside those of Constantine a century later. They made the capital city virtually impenetrable. The city walls of Theodosius would be overcome only twice by enemy force, by the Crusaders in 1204 and the Turks in 1453. After the Turkish victory, the name was changed to Istanbul. Large sections of those impressive fortifications remain in Istanbul to this day.

Busy trade routes led from Constantinople

Portrait of a Byzantine noblewoman from the fourth century

The citizens of Constantinople were very proud of their newly founded city. On this coin the city is depicted as a female.

1046

Ivory plaque depicting an Eastern Roman emperor from the fourth century

1047

to Asia Minor and the west. The spacious harbors were filled with commercial ships. Location and official protection had made Byzantium the meeting place of east and west and became known, justifiably, as the *emporium*, the commercial center of the world.

From its very inception, the city had been meant to be a second Rome. Hence, Constantinople was given an administrative organization modeled after that of the old capital, complete with a state prefect and a senate. It became the autonomous center of the empire. Its large population, provided with grain at city expense, was accommodated in planned housing.

However, Constantinople clearly differed from the old Roman capital in several aspects. The city was not Latin, but Greek in both language and culture, and the new capital was Christian from its very beginning. There was no room for pagan temples in Constantine's city. His residence became a city of churches. Unlike Rome, which developed spontaneously, Constantinople was planned, using the framework of Byzantium. The new capital was intended to avoid the criss-crossing nightmare of alleys, *insulae* (public apartment houses), markets, arches, and temples of Rome. Constantinople was to become a reflection of imperial might. Its architects designed a well-organized street plan with large squares, broad avenues, and precisely calculated building lines. They designed horizontally, not vertically. Often the dwellings were several stories high, but real insulae on the Roman model were never built.

However, behind the main streets, private builders went their own way, especially after the death of Constantine. The result, despite the plan, was chaos. Quite soon, a tangle of small streets and alleyways stretched over the hills, interrupted here and there by tiny squares where neighborhood merchants loudly advertised their wares. The main building materials were clay, straw, and wood. Construction was rarely solid and certainly unable to withstand the frequent earthquakes. These invariably created fires, which spread readily from roof to roof, destroying entire neighborhoods. Fighting the fires was impossible. The little pails and the primitive wooden hand pumps available were no match for the conflagrations. Water, however, was never lacking.

Emperor Valens (ruling from 364 to 378) had built an impressive aqueduct using stones taken from Chalcedon. (This was an ancient Greek seaport across from

Honorius, the son of the emperor Theodosius, was emperor of the Western Roman Empire from 395 to 423.

Byzantine chalice from the tenth century, decorated with cloisonné enamel

A large network of pipelines and aqueducts transported water to the city of Constantinople, where it was kept in large reservoirs. This Medusa head forms the basis of one of the 336 columns in an underground cistern in Constantinople that was built in the sixth century.

Constantinople on the Sea of Marmara. It had been a Roman possession since the first century BC.) The aqueduct did not lead directly to the fountains and bathhouses. Valens had tremendous reservoirs in cisterns carved out of the rocks beneath the city. Some of these were entirely underground, but their supporting pillars, which would never be seen except by torchlight, were lavishly decorated. The reservoirs guaranteed the city a supply of water even if the aqueduct were cut.

### Administration

Constantinople was divided into fourteen districts, each with its own administration. Neighborhood officials were responsible for public services and public order. Each neighborhood developed its own characteristics; a

Constantinople soon grew into a large metropolis. This twelfth-century miniature shows houses several stories high along a street in Constantinople.

person was characterized by his neighborhood. The ideal of every Byzantine citizen was to own a villa in District IV, the royal quarter. The elite lived there, clustered around the impressive complex of the court which set the destiny of the city. The royal palace grew, over time, into a small city. Its churches, chancelleries, the villas of court dignitaries, and the harbor basin formed an impressive complex. Beautiful gardens surrounded the palaces and marble arcades connected the buildings. Corrupt ministers, ladies of the court, calculating eunuchs, and power-hungry *prelates* (church officials) schemed for favor from the emperor.

Constantinople had the atmosphere of a frontier city. Constantine had called adventurers from all over the empire to his new capital. Perhaps some of their pioneer spirit lived on in the character of the people. The language of the streets was Greek. Most of the populace came from the eastern part of the empire, with Greek and Syrian elements predominating.

## The Nika Revolt

Emperor Anastasius had been a fervent supporter of the Greens. His successor Justin I was a member of the Blue faction, which proclaimed differing religious beliefs. The future emperor, Justinian I, who had followed his imperial uncle into the Blues, was an orthodox Christian on a mission to restore orthodoxy. The competition between the two factions was stronger than ever during those years. Inheriting the throne from Justin I in 527, Justinian I attempted to placate the opposition by no longer standing unconditionally behind the Blues. His attempt to manage the two parties, at least to some extent, achieved little.

In 532, a few ringleaders from each of the two groups were arrested and imprisoned. This was met by public rebellion. The parties joined together against the emperor. The situation evolved into the greatest crisis in Justinian's long reign.

In the Hippodrome, on Tuesday, January 13, 532, the groups jointly demanded the release of the prisoners. The emperor did not respond. In the evening following the races, a huge throng of people assembled in the heart of the city, shouting "Nika! Nika!" What once was the call of the racetrack was now the battle cry of a rebel movement. Dissidents started fires. Many buildings, including the *Hagia Sophia*, were burned to the ground. The next day in the Hippodrome, the groups demanded the dismissal of three ministers they despised. The rebellion had taken a clear political turn. Deciding that the only way he could get out of this situation was to give in quickly, he announced his agreement to the demands.

This had precisely the wrong effect. The people now went even further. They demanded no less than the resignation of the emperor. Hypatios, a nephew of the former emperor Anastasius, was acclaimed the new emperor amid loud cheering in the Hippodrome. On Sunday, January 18, Justinian once again faced the people at the racetrack. People called him a pig, yelling out "Long live Hypatios." All of Constantinople was in the hands of the rebels. At his residence, Justinian consulted with Belisarius, his most important general, as well as with the ministers who had just called for his ousting. All the dignitaries advised the emperor to run while he still

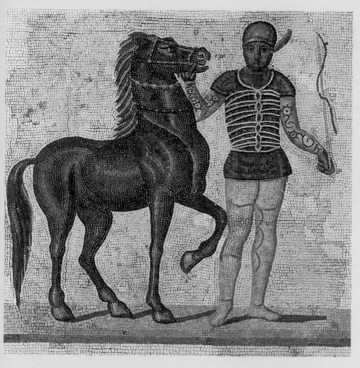

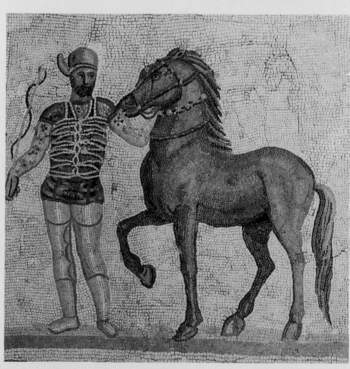

could. He could leave the palace by a back door and descend, unseen, to a boat moored in the harbor. Just as Justinian was about to take this advice, Empress Theodora entered the room. She said, "We all have to die sometime, but a person who has been emperor cannot live without the robes of royalty. If you wish to save your life by fleeing, this is not difficult: there is the harbor, and there are the ships. I agree with the old saying that royal purple makes a beautiful shroud."

These words stimulated a change of plans. In response to a report that the masses in the racetracks were in disagreement with each other, a decision was made to risk military action. General Belisarius and his Germanics entered the Hippodrome, where the masses proved unable to fight, too densely packed together. Belisarius massacred 30,000 of them. The Nika revolt had been squelched in blood.

Roman mosaic from the fifth century, on which the four different teams of a chariot race can be seen. The supporters dressed in the colors of their favorite team (green, red, yellow, or blue).

## City Center

At the center of the city was the square called the Augustaion, named by its founder after his mother, Augusta Helena. The bronze gate to the palaces was there, and *Hagia Sophia* (the Church of Holy Wisdom), the senate, and the horse racetrack, the Hippodrome. The *Mesè* (main street) poured its flood of humanity into the square from a great distance, up to the Golden Gate in Constantine's city walls. On both sides, galleries protected strollers from the sun. Huge courtyards alternated with the porticos. The Mesè was without question the most important street in the entire empire. Goods from all corners of the world were displayed there and every craft was practiced under the porticos. At night, the Mesè showed the other face of the metropolis. Then the same galleries under the porticos were the domain of sleeping beggars. Constantinople's grandeur was a facade. The masses lived in misery, often kept alive only by the grain distributed by the emperor.

Constantinople still practiced the traditional distribution of grain to every registered father of a family. However, the court made attempts to control other food prices. In general, there were enough supplies in the city, but occasional catastrophic outbreaks of famine occurred.

This was dangerous, because 200,000 hungry people posed an enormous threat to the stability of the government. The people of Constantinople were restless, quick to anger and to fight. They enjoyed the horse racing Constantine had imported from Rome. The Hippodrome, the largest racetrack of the city, had room for 50,000 spectators. Among them were usually the emperor and his peers. He sat above the stalls in the Kathisma, the royal box, which was directly connected to the royal palace. To the ordinary man, the Kathisma was the center of political life. In the anonymity of the Hippodrome, individuals could freely air their views by cheering for the emperor horse, or a challenger. The races served as both a political and an emotional outlet for the public.

## Green *versus* Blue

The organization of the games was in the hands of two clubs, the Greens and the Blues. Over the years, they had developed

A farmer returns from the land. Mosaic from the imperial palace in Constantinople (fifth and sixth centuries)

The shepherd was a Roman symbol of charity, adopted by Christians as a symbol for the benevolent Christ. Mosaic from the imperial palace

into powerful syndicates which organized all entertainment in the Hippodrome. Charioteers, trainers, grooms, and stable hands all belonged to one of them. Every Byzantine citizen supported either the Greens or the Blues. The jockeys appeared on the track dressed in either green or blue colors. The odds in the Hippodrome were the chief topic of conversation. The competition was tough and the races often ended in bloody riots.

The two clubs had also acquired administrative and political importance. In case of emergency, they could mobilize the population to guard the city walls. Organization then was in the hands of the club officials. The parties differed in social composition, and political and religious preferences. The Blues were said to be orthodox Christians, oriented to a rural and traditional lifestyle. The Greens found their followers among the merchants and the lower classes of people. Being a supporter, however, was largely an emotional matter. It was also not always clear what each of the two parties wanted, apart from triumphing over the other.

The emperor in the Kathisma had to attune himself to the sensitivities of the Greens and the Blues. The court was generally sympathetic to the Blues, although a sensible ruler generally kept the parties so busy that they could not turn against the government. The most important races took place on Christmas Day and on May 11 (the founding date of Constantinople as the capital city). On those days, the streets were deserted and the cry of *nika* (conquer) resounded from the Hippodrome. Troops waited behind the great sports arena, ready to subdue any possible outbursts. If things failed to go their way, the emperor's supporters might suddenly prove to be revolutionaries.

The emperor's might was based, to some extent, upon the agreement of the people. Some emperors came to power only after public riots in their favor. Some emperors came to power through palace revolutions, others by conspiracy or by the choice of the widow of a deceased ruler. An orderly system of succession existed only in theory. Some emperors trained a favorite as successor. Others left the question to their survivors. There was no organized system of voting and no civil code. After an intended new emperor managed to gain palace favor, he would have himself acclaimed emperor in the Hippodrome. Only then would he be given the outward trappings of his power from the hands of the *patriarch* (head of the church), letting the people know his position. In the popular view, the emperor was considered God's chosen one, obligated only to God for his position. However, this did not take away from the fact that subjects would often endeavor to overthrow the emperor. The thinking was that, were such an attempt to be successful, success would be proof that God had switched support to the usurper. Hence, the position of the emperor was always precarious, making Constantinople a troubled and dangerous city.

Ivory diptych of Boethius, who was consul in Rome in the year 487

## Anastasius I, the Monophysite (ca. 430–518)

The greatest passion of the Byzantines, second only to horse racing, was theology. Ever since doctrinal questions raised by the Arian controversy in the fourth century, popular interest had existed in theology. Even craftsmen found themselves embroiled in theological debates. The doctrines of Arius (a fourth-century theologian from Libya) taught that Jesus was not of the same substance as God, but only the best of created beings. This was considered heresy in Rome

1053

Originally, Venice was a Byzantine city. The basilica of San Marco was built after the example of the Church of Hagia Sophia in Constantinople.

and condemned in 325 at the first ecumenical council at Nicaea. Arius was reinstated in the east by Emperor Constantine I in 334 and supported by Emperor Constantius II and Eusebius of Nicomedia, patriarch (head of the Orthodox Church). In 359, Arian Christianity was made the state religion. Constantius II died in 361, succeeded by anti-Arian emperors Valens and then Theodosius. In 379, Theodosius accepted the Nicene Creed. Its principles, condemning Arianism, were adopted by the second ecumenical council in 381.

The greatest point of contention in the fifth and sixth centuries continued to be the divinity of Christ. The issue this time was the doctrine of *Monophysitism*. The word comes from the Greek *monos* (single) and *physis* (nature). According to it, Jesus Christ had only a single nature, which was divine, not human. This conflicted with the orthodox doctrine that Christ was at once divine and human. In 451, Pope Leo I convened the fourth ecumenical gathering of the Christian church in Chalcedon to resolve the contro-

versy. The edict of the Council of Chalcedon failed to reconcile the opposing views. (In the sixth century, the Monophysites would secede from the parent church. Condemned at the sixth ecumenical council in 681, Monophysitism continues today in the Abyssinian, Armenian, Coptic, and Jacobite churches.)

Meanwhile, in the east, the debate raged. The people of Syria and the Egyptian countryside nearly all opted for the Monophysitic concept. In Constantinople, there was no consensus. The Monophysites found many advocates among the lower classes, but had influence even in the highest ranks. Emperor Anastasius (who ruled between 491 and 518) was counted as one of their members.

Interior of the Hagia Sophia in ❯ Constantinople. After the Nika revolt, Justinian had the church rebuilt between 532 and 537. It is the largest and most sophisticated domed church in the world. In 1453, when the city was conquered by the Muslims, the church was turned into a mosque.

1055

Part of an ivory diptych on which a chariot race in the Hippodrome of Constantinople can be seen. The emperor watches the race from his private viewing area.

mass. The Blues were shocked and infuriated. After the service, they called for a new emperor. Fights broke out with the Greens. Within a few days, the entire city was in an uproar. Rioting people set fire to the houses of the emperor's family and called for the orthodox general Areobindus to intervene. The general, however, had no desire to lead the rebels and left town.

Anastasius I decided to confront his people. Dressed in simple clothes and without his crown, he appeared in the Kathisma, where 20,000 rebels booed him. The emperor humbly asked for forgiveness, even offering to resign. The people were dumbfounded. People paid to cheer, posted among the rebels, yelled, "Long live Anastasius." What could have been his downfall became a triumph for Anastasius. He promised religious concessions and withdrew into the palace. The rebels went quietly home. That same day, Anastasius I began making a series of arrests. He had divided the revolutionaries and he now began his revenge. The instigators paid for their insurgency with their lives as the emperor resumed his old politics more strongly than ever.

Anastasius I had been made emperor after the death of Zeno in 491, marrying Zeno's widow the same year. His popularity with the people had already been in some question before his public support of the Monophysitic doctrine. He was notable for his effort to eliminate the widely enjoyed stadium combats between gladiators and wild animals. He had also tried to abolish some very popular dances, which he considered immoral. He was famous for military discipline as well, developing a strong army that he used often. His foreign affairs were plagued with battle, first against the rebelling Isaurians, then Persia, and finally, against invading Slavs and Huns and his fellow Europeans, the Bulgars. (Anastasius was born in Dyrrhachium, in today's Albania.)

The insurrection against Anastasius ran a course which followed a frequent pattern in Constantinople. Religious dissent would lead to an outburst. The emperor would silence the masses with empty promises and then would take his revenge. The people, as was evident in 512, were capable of dangerous rebellion, but the situation was frequently too spontaneous, too badly coordinated to be successful. The masses were mercurial in their convictions, changing sides rapidly. The opponents of Anastasius were an example. One day the Blues wanted to burn down half the city; the next day, they cheered their heretical leader enthusiastically. A far bloodier rebellion in 532, the Nika rebellion, would end essentially the same way.

Although he was a layman, he had voiced his beliefs in his scholarly sermons before taking the throne. Throughout his reign, he supported the Monophysites wherever possible. The Blue party opposed him. In 512, there were violent uprisings. On Sunday, November 4, 512, the priest in the Hagia Sophia offered up a Monophysitic prayer during

Picture of a mosaic in the Church of Hagia Sophia in Istanbul (formerly Constantinople). The Virgin Mary, with the infant Jesus on her lap, sits in the center of the picture. To the left and right Constantine the Great and Emperor Justinian are depicted. They offer her the city of Constantinople and the Church of Hagia Sophia.

# The Rule of Justinian

## The Eastern Roman Empire as a Power

The situation in the Eastern Roman Empire in the turbulent fifth century was little better than that in Ravenna, where the western sovereigns had settled. The throne in both empires had become an unstable position, subject to the manipulations of conspirators. The young sons of Theodosius I had inherited the title, Honorius (at age twelve) in the west and Arcadius (at eighteen) in the east. Theodosius had appointed the Roman general Flavius Stilicho, an honest and intelligent man, as regent for Honorius, stabilizing the Western Empire. The court at Constantinople, in contrast, was plagued by intrigue and no strong leader prevailed among the ambitious and often unscrupulous contenders.

In 400, the Goth Gainas, an ambitious general in mercenary service in the Eastern Empire, attempted to gain power similar to that held by Stilicho in the west. He managed to turn the entire court, not least of all the empress Eudoxia, against him. Gainas was detested by the general public, as well, partly for reasons of religion. Like the Goths he

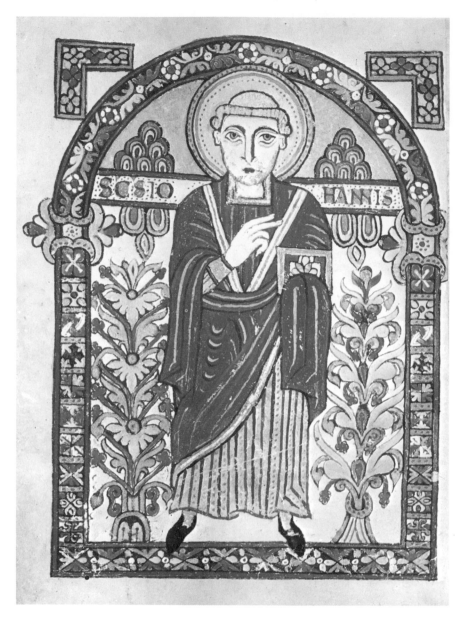

Miniature from
the ninth century, depicting
Bishop John Chrysostom
(Golden Mouth)

led, he professed the Arian version of Christianity. In the Greek view, this made them not only uncivilized barbarians, but heretical. The citizens of Constantinople, led by the Imperial Guard and probably encouraged by the senate, rose up against Gainas and slaughtered thousands of Goths and soldiers. Gainas was killed as a result, but the circumstances of his death are disputed.

In consequence, the Eastern Roman court decided that it would no longer give the army command to foreigners. The empire drew its troops from among its own subjects, notably the Isaurian mountain people from the south of Asia Minor. The "barbarians" were, in fact, a permanant part of the empire.

### Theodosius II (?–450)

Theodosius II, son of Arcadius, was only a child when he ascended the throne in 408. Throughout his life, power remained in the hands of a corrupt court clique comprising eunuchs, princesses, ministers, and prelates.

They ran the empire for their own profit. The only exception was Pulcheria, sister of the emperor. She exerted such influence from her convent that the choice of a successor to Theodosius, in 450, was left to her discretion. The man she chose was an officer named Marcian (reigned 450–457), whom Pulcheria married *pro forma* (in form only) without giving up her celibate life.

The Eastern Roman Empire survived the tempestuous years of the fifth century rela-

2 cel fum dejcur. Soluuq; fimixumm ...

Totila, the leader of the
Ostrogoths, pays a visit to
St. Benedict. Miniature
from a manuscript that is kept
in the library of the Vatican

tively unscathed. The huge stream of migrating Gothic and Hunnish peoples flowed mainly west. Since Alaric, no one had presented a serious threat to the Eastern Empire. Its enemies were primarily interested in spoils and could usually be bought off. Immigrants were still permitted to enter the empire at the Danube border. Emperor Marcian gave the Ostrogoths land in Pannonia. The traditional enemy Persia continued to be a threat on the eastern border, but was less aggressive in the fifth century than in the past.

The essential nature of the east-west conflict remained unchanged. The two imperial powers tried to snatch provincial states from each other, which led to generally short-lived battles.

### Theodoric the Great (ca. 454–526)
The Eastern Roman Empire had continued difficulty with the Ostrogothic warriors they

had permitted to enter the empire as foederati. In 483, they united under their king Theodoric, posing a considerable threat to imperial authority. From Emperor Zeno (who ruled from 474 to 491), the Goth had

The Church of Sant' Apollinare Nuovo in Ravenna (Italy). It was the palace chapel of Theodoric. The bell tower is of later date. The city of Ravenna was the residence of the last emperors of the Western Roman Empire.

acquired land for his people as well as a general command in the service of Byzantium.

Born in the Roman province of Pannonia, Theodoric had been raised as a hostage at the Byzantine court from the age of seven to seventeen. Selected by his tribe as king after his father was killed by the Huns in battle in 474, Theodoric fought and then allied with the Byzantine emperor Zeno. In 488, Theodoric requested permission to take over Italy. The emperor promptly agreed. The further away the Ostrogoths were, the better. The Herulian Odoacer ruled Italy as "king of the Germanics," with no intention of yielding his throne. After Theodoric invaded, he offered valiant resistance for five years, finally surrendering after three decisive battles and a long blockade of his capital, Ravenna. In 493, when the rest of Italy had been taken by Theodoric, Odoacer agreed to joint rule. Before the year was out, Theodoric had his new-found colleague and all of his followers slaughtered. The Ostrogoth military conference hoisted Theodoric onto his shield, naming him king of Italy.

Theodoric ruled for the next thirty-three years, an era of great peace. Following the example of Roman civilization, he formed a peaceful society where Goths and Romans could live in harmony with one another. He used separate laws for the two peoples, cooperating with the Roman Senate. He gave Romans high command in his army. He let the Romans run their own government and gave them positions at his court. It was Theodoric's dream to have a revived Latin culture within his Gothic Kingdom.

Religion was the primary obstacle to a positive relationship between the Goths and the Romans. The Ostrogoths were Arians, rejecting the traditional Christian concept that Jesus Christ and God were of the same substance. This put them in some conflict with not only the pope in Rome but the anti-Arian emperor Justinian I in Constantinople.

## Justinian I, the Great (483–565)

The Illyrian Flavius Petrus Sabgatius Justinianus, called Justinian I, the Great, ascended the throne of Constantinople in 518. He was named as fellow ruler by his reigning uncle Justin. He had grand plans to put the fragmented empire back together. He wanted the western regions taken by Germanic invaders in the past century returned to Roman sovereignty and the Germanic kings reduced to subordinate status. He felt they should see Byzantine troops, not Byzantine money. His goal of a reunited empire was a religious necessity.

Since the fourth century, Christianity had been inseparably connected with the empire. In the new emperor's view, there could only be one God and only one emperor. Justinian's slogan, "One empire, one law, one church," dictated the policy of his government. He attempted, without success, to reconcile the religious arguments between the Monophysites and the Orthodox Christian Church.

The Monophysites refused all compromise and organized their own underground church in the eastern section of Justinian's empire.

Known as "the emperor who never sleeps," Justinian worked day and night, if not on legislation, then on the writing of theological tracts. However, laws and tracts were not sufficient to achieve his purpose. The restoration of the empire demanded both war and the suppression of domestic dissent. Justinian left both tasks largely to his general Belisarius but also permitted his wife a significant voice in matters of government.

The emperor married the actress and courtesan Theodora in 523, making her his joint ruler when he took full power on the death of Justin in 527. Justinian flouted tradition when he married Theodora, who was not of royal blood, but intelligent and principled, with a clear understanding of politics.

In 532, when the popular rebellion called the Nika riot broke out on the streets of Constantinople, she persuaded

The Church of San Vitale in Ravenna

"The Prophet Ezra Rewriting Sacred Records," from the *Codex Amiatinex*, written in Northumbria around 750

1061

Justinian to remain as emperor. The same year, the eastern border of the empire was rendered safe by a peace treaty with Persia, but elsewhere, military intervention was seen as necessary.

## Justinian's Campaigns
### North Africa

Justinian had been presented with the impetus for intervention in North Africa in 530. In the Vandal Kingdom at Carthage, noblemen killed their pro-Roman king right after he had appealed to Constantinople for assistance. They replaced him with an anti-Roman king. In 533, Belisarius and his army made a surprise attack on the African coast with the intent of reasserting imperial authority.

The Arian Vandals proved to be without support in the immense country. The farmers were not interested in war. The city dwellers, supported by Constantinople, openly chose the Romans. Carthage drove out its Arian rulers. While orthodox clergymen took over the churches, celebrating people illuminated the town ramparts. They greeted imperial troops as liberators, although Belisarius had a hard time stopping his soldiers from plun-

The Church of Hagia Sophia was lavishly decorated. This upper part of a column bears the initials of Empress Theodora, wife of Emperor Justinian.

One of the famous mosaics in the church of San Vitale in Ravenna. In the center stands Emperor Justinian. Next to him is Maximianus, bishop of Ravenna, whose name is written above him. The others are lower clergy and soldiers.

dering. Within a year, all Vandal resistance was broken. The Vandal Kingdom in North Africa was reincorporated into the empire in 534. In Constantinople, a triumphant parade was held. In the Hippodrome, the Vandal king was forced to kneel before Justinian while the people cheered.

As part of the same campaign, Belisarius and his troops occupied the Mediterranean islands of Sardinia, Corsica, and the Balearics without resistance.

The church of Saint Irene in Constantinople (present-day Istanbul). It was built during the reign of Emperor Justinian.

### Italy

The following year, it was Italy's turn. A dynastic conflict cleared the way for Constantinople's intervention. Belisarius landed on Sicily, took over the island without a fight and proceeded to attack the Ostrogoths on the Italian mainland. For the next twenty years, war continued in Italy. What had been presented by the east as a battle of liberation ended in senseless violence, tyranny, and exploitation. The nonstop fighting took its toll on discipline. The soldiers from Constantinople were feared everywhere, the governors despised, the officials scorned.

Rome was repeatedly occupied. Outside it, the Ostrogoths blocked the water supply,

## Theodora (ca. 508–548)

Empress Theodora was not raised in royal circles. Her father was a bear tamer in the Hippodrome, who worked for the Green party. This put him in the lowest rank of society. People who earned a living by providing some form of amusement were viewed with contempt in Constantinople. Actors and actresses, in particular, were seen as immoral. Little differentiation was made between actresses and prostitutes, with some justification, given the standard practices of the time. Even the law had been adapted to such thinking. For example, sons of actresses could not become bishops and senators.

When her father died, Theodora was still a child. Her mother remarried immediately. Her intent was to give her new husband the just-vacated position of bear tamer and to secure a future for herself and her children. However, the Green party had already been bribed to give the job to another candidate. Hunger threatened the family. Fortunately, Theodora's mother received permission to display her sad state to the public in the Hippodrome. Blanketed with flowers, she and her children begged for help during the break between parts of the program. The Blues claimed to be moved by such a sorry tale of Green corruption. They arranged a job for Theodora's stepfather, something which the later empress never forgot. For the rest of her life, she remained a fervent supporter of the Blues. Meanwhile, she learned the only trade still open to her: acting. She became a pantomime artist, the stage long being the province of balletlike pantomime presentations.

It was the racier scenes that made Theodora well known, such as the portrayal

destroying the ancient aqueducts. Rome's famous baths were dry. The old capital collapsed. Nevertheless, its occupation by the Goths was unsuccessful. When they withdrew, the war took a turn in favor of the Byzantines. In 540, with Belisarius's takeover of the Ravenna residence, it appeared that the Gothic resistance had been broken. The general was transferred to the east, urgently needed to battle the Persian armies.

Within a year, Italy was again ablaze. The

Mosaic in the Church
of San Vitale in Ravenna
depicting Empress
Theodora with her ladies-in-
waiting and two clerics.
She was the influential wife
of Emperor Justinian.

of the myth of Leda, to whom Zeus made love to in the guise of a swan. Theodora acquired throngs of admirers. Her first step into the world of the elite came when a high official took her as his mistress, but the affair ended with Theodora turned out on the street. When she eventually met Justinian, it was love at first sight, but the law prevented the marriage of an emperor to a courtesan.

However, for the nephew and future successor of the then-emperor Justin I, this proved no real obstacle. Justinian had his uncle rescind the rules banning marriage with an actress. A short time later, the couple were married by the patriarch of Constantinople. Two years later Theodora was made empress.

She played her new role with enthusiasm. Extraordinarily intelligent and strong-willed, she captivated the court. On occasion, she even worked against her husband, protecting the Monophysites, for example. During the Nika revolt in 532, she enabled the emperor to keep the throne. She died in 547, leaving a disconsolate seventy-seven-year-old husband.

Ostrogoths found a new leader in Totila, who demonstrated great talent as a general and as a politician. The Romans had come to loathe the liberation of Belisarius and the horde of corrupt officials that had swarmed over the country with the Byzantine armies. These included the financial expert Alexander, popularly known as "the Scissors." Totila promised deliverance from the Scissors and his henchmen. He also promised freedom to the slaves and land distribution to all. In three years, he had driven out the Byzantines and undone the accomplishments of Belisarius.

The Byzantine general had been ordered to reconquer the lost territories, but he had gotten no further than beleaguered Rome. After a few years, Belarius resigned. Justinian replaced him with the old eunuch Narses, who had proven his military capacities as commander of the palace guard. In 552, he marched into Italy with a large army that included many Germanic soldiers. Totila was killed in a terrible battle. By 553, the last Gothic resistance had been broken.

The Arian Baptistry
in Ravenna,
built at the beginning of the
sixth century

Decoration in the
dome of the Arian Baptistry.
The center of the mosaic
depicts Christ baptized
by John the Baptist.
Around this scene a procession
of the twelve apostles
is depicted.

The Italy that Narses offered to his emperor was impoverished and exhausted. Its population hated the new rulers and their tax policies. Rome, the eternal city, was demolished. The water that flowed from the smashed aqueducts turned the surrounding countryside into an unhealthy swampland. The marble statues that had once decorated the *fora* (city squares) were broken and used as projectiles against the Goths. The famous *thermae* (baths) would never function again. The Circus Maximus was abandoned. The destruction was irreversible. The city would remain in ruins throughout the Middle Ages.

### Southern Spain

Conflicts in the Visigothic Kingdom gave Justinian an excuse to intervene there. In 550, he began a third campaign, landing an army in southeastern Spain. The troops succeeded in reconquering the coastal area but got no further. The Visigoths united against them, blocking further advance.

Spain was Justinian's last conquest. He had regained most of the lands on the perimeter of the Mediterranean that had once been Roman. Only Gaul and northern Spain remained outside his control. He could find no more armies to do the job. When he died, in 565, over eighty years old, the empire had difficulty just keeping its borders intact, despite the fortifications the emperor had built. The Persian War had resumed in 540 and the Slavs had begun to encroach in the Balkan Peninsula.

### The Justinian Code

Justinian's name is not associated exclusively with his wars of conquest and his efforts to reunite the Roman Empire. He gained lasting fame from his extensive codification of the imperial legal system. There was a great need for systematization of the laws in the centralized empire he wanted. The emperor took his self-imposed task very seriously, working at all hours among his documents and papers of state. He created a commission of legal scholars to help him, appointing the jurist Trebonianus to direct it. Trebonianus was a pagan, which made it possible for him to remain outside the fierce religious battles. Although the emperor himself was a notable persecutor of pagans, he did not attempt to convert the scholar or to correct his infamous corruption. Justinian needed his talent too much.

It took the team a decade to organize the enormous number of laws and the chaos of imperial jurisprudence, yet it is chiefly due to Trebonianus's organizational skills that the work came into being even that rapidly. The final product was made part of the enormous *Corpus Juris Civilis* (*Body of Civil Law*). Completed in 534, it was also called the *Codex Justinianus* (*Justinian Code*).

The *Corpus Juris* consisted of three parts. The first was a compilation of all imperial laws still valid since the government of Hadrian. The second, called the *Digesta*, was a summary of the legal tracts of the great Roman legal scholars from the time of the emperors. (This remains, today, one of the best sources of information on Roman law.) The third part, the *Institutiones* (*Institutions*) was an introduction to law for students. The entire document, promulgated (approved by legislative authority) in 534, was periodically updated by the inclusion of new decrees, or *Novellae*. The code itself represents one of the greatest intellectual accomplishments of the century.

Like any code in jurisprudence, the *Corpus Juris Civilis* was a systematic compilation of previously written statutes, although it was not arranged into criminal or civil branches. Its influence would outlive the empire, constituting the basis for civil

Throne of Bishop
Maximianus of Ravenna.
The chair is made of
carved ivory.

Ruins of a
Byzantine church
in Carthage,
Tunisia

1067

law in much of the western world. It served as the foundation for the laws of most European countries. Through a Spanish version of it called *Siete Partidas* (*Seven Parts*), the code also became the basis for law in most of the nations of Latin America.

If the *Corpus Juris* was a legal monument to Justinian's rule, Hagia Sophia, the Church of Holy Wisdom, was a concrete one. To this day, its great dome rises above the skyline of Istanbul. For 1,400 years, the building has

Interior of the Church of Sant' Apollinare near Ravenna. This church was built in the sixth century.

survived all kinds of disasters. Constantine the Great had built the first Hagia Sophia, but it was burned to the ground in the Nika Rebellion of 532. Justinian decided to forgo yet another restoration and built a new and larger building to the glory of God, the empire, and his own rule. His architects Anthemius of Tralles and Isidorus of Miletus researched all prior building techniques they could find before undertaking construction of the new church. They designed a huge central dome 185 feet (56 meters) high over a circle of windows on a square base. They used four curved triangles, called pendentives, to carry support to the dome, by transferring its weight through four massive arches to the square base of the structure. Such a transition between dome and base had never been built before and constituted a major innovation in architecture. Thanks to the

combined efforts of thousands of workmen, the edifice was completed between 532 and 537. As in all Byzantine architecture, the exterior of the church is plain. Because the supports can only be seen on the outside of the church, the dome appears to hang suspended on a halo of light coming through a circle of windows. The interior is exquisitely decorated with mosaics and polished marble. Justinian said in awe, "Solomon, I have outdone thee!" referring to the temple built by Solomon in Jerusalem. The church, made a mosque by the Ottomans in 1453, is now a museum.

During an earthquake a few years after its construction, the original dome collapsed. Justinian ordered new calculations made and a sturdier dome built. That one, dating from 563, still graces the church today.

Historians disagree about Justinian's politics. Some of them claim he was a great politician; others call him a fanatic for trying to realize the dream of a world-encompassing empire. Justinian wanted to renew a decayed structure; in this view, and in his attempt, he did more harm than good, exhausting the realm with innumerable wars. Subsequent generations would have to pay the bill. Still other critics maintain that the Eastern Roman Empire outgrew its own power under Justinian's rule. They claim that he failed to understand his time and unnecessarily incurred an impressive range of enemies. The latter view is not without justification. What Justinian established was a comprehensive military system, not a unit. The old territories of imperial Rome had long ceased to be a single unit. The migration of Germanic peoples could not be undone, nor could the impoverishment and population decreases of the western provinces be readily repaired. The financial cost of the many armies and the innumerable fortifications could simply no longer be met. In any case, Justinian represented the end of an era. Byzantine power began to crumble almost immediately after his death.

Yet new enemies were already waiting in the wings. The Avers, a people related to the Huns, appeared in 568 in southern Russia and in the Balkans, driving the Lombards into Italy. At the same time, the Slavs crossed the Danube to the south in great numbers. Before the end of the sixth century, they would represent the greatest part of the population of the Balkans.

Shortly thereafter, in the seventh century, the Arabs would begin their march of triumph in Asia and Africa. The holdings of the Roman Empire would dwindle to not much more than Asia Minor and a few bridgeheads in Europe.

Relief from Naksh-i-Rustam near Persepolis. Ahura Mazda offers the crown to Ardashir. In the meantime both crush their enemies: Ahura Mazda slaughters Ariman, and Ardashir tramples Artabanus.

# The New Persian Empire

## *The Restoration of Old Glory*

The kingdom of Parthia, located in today's Iran and Afghanistan, was founded about 250 BC. By the first century BC, it had become an extensive empire that ran from the Euphrates River in Mesopotamia east to the Indus River. From the Amu Darya River in the north, it ran south to the Indian Ocean. Subjected in turn by the Assyrians, the Medes, the Persians, the Macedonians (under Alexander the Great), and the Seleucids, by the middle of the first century BC Parthia was the rival of the Roman Empire. In the second century AD it suffered defeat, first by the Roman emperor Trajan and then by Lucius Verus, coemperor with Marcus Aurelius. At the beginning of the third century, Parthia was conquered by

the Roman emperor Lucius Septimius Severus.

### Ardashir I (?-AD 241)

In 226, Ardashir I, governor of the province of Persia, revolted. Reigning over a part of the traditional homeland of the Persians, he was no foreigner. His grandfather Sassan, for whom a dynasty was named, had been a priest of the Persian god Ahura Mazda. His father, a vassal of the king of Parthia, had appointed himself district governor. In 212, Ardashir assumed that position after his father died. For a dozen years, he battled opposing royal vassals for supremacy, killing his own brothers to obtain it. The Persians enthusiastically joined the rebellious leader. In 224, he overthrew Artabanus V, the king of Parthia, at the Battle of Hormuz and gave himself the title of king of kings. Thus began the New Persian Empire under the dynasty of the Sassanids.

Ardashir I attempted to restore the Persian Empire to the glory it had once had under the Achaemenids. This was the dynasty that had ruled Persia from about 550 BC to 330 BC, named for the seventh-century ruler Achaemenes. His great-great-grandson, Cyrus the Great, had, in fact, created both the dynasty and the Persian Empire, which reached its peak under Darius I, the Great.

The Achaemenid dynasty created an excellent system of public administration, codified its laws, and established both reliable currency and mail service. Its members were usually Zoroastrian but tolerant of other religions. They were noted for their encouragement of the arts, literature, and architecture. The dy-

Remains of the royal palace at Ctesiphon, which was probably built under Shapur I. These are the remnants of the great *iwan*, a hall with an arched ceiling. The room was open at the front and closed at the back.

nasty ended in 330 BC with the death of Darius III. Ardashir, claiming to have descended from Darius and the great Persian kings, saw himself as its direct successor. Ardashir established a new dynasty, naming it Sassanid after his grandfather. His idols had been Zoroastrian; hence, he made Zoroastrianism the national religion of this New Persian Empire.

The new king made a new capital at the ancient Mesopotamian city of Ctesiphon on the Tigris River. It had been the winter residence and eventually the capital of the Parthian kings. He went on to conquer adja-

cent kingdoms and, farther away, Armenia. He also invaded the Punjab region of India, exacting tribute from its rulers.

### Shapur I (?-AD 272)

In 240, Ardashir left a consolidated empire to his son Shapur I, who expanded his power to the Himalayas. He then undertook to fulfill a promise made to his father to conquer the Romans. In two wars, he seized territory in Mesopotamia, Syria, and Asia Minor. In 260, he reached Antioch, where he devastated the Roman emperor Valerian and his army. Valerian ended his life as Shapur's footstool.

Shapur I took the Roman emperor Valerian prisoner, and used him as his footstool from that moment onward. Contemporary relief from Naksh-i-Rustam

In fact, after his death, the king had him stuffed with straw so that he could continue to serve.

En route back to Persia between 260 and 263, Shapur suffered serious losses at the hands of the troops of Odenathus, prince of Palmyra and an ally of Rome. The only fruit

Tower
in Naksh-i-Rustam,
built in the
fifth century AD

of his western campaigns was the vassal state of Armenia. In addition, his campaigns had brought thousands of prisoners of war to Mesopotamia, among them scores of Syrian Christians. The expansion of Christianity in the Persian Empire, begun under the Parthians, was thus inadvertently stimulated. Despite occasional persecution, Christianity gradually spread.

Shapur organized a compilation of the Zend-Avesta, the prayer books of Zoroa-strianism. Also called the *Avesta*, these sacred books are a record of early Persian customs. Shapur had fragments from Greek papers on medicine, astronomy, and meta-physics added to the work. After the fourth-century BC conquest of Persia by Alexander the Great, most of the books were lost. Shapur's revisions would be destroyed again in the seventh century AD by Muslims taking over Persia and forcibly converting the Zoroastrians, many of whom fled to India, taking their scripture with them.

All kinds of old eastern religious cults, some influenced by Greco-Roman concepts, existed in the Persian Empire side by side with Zoroastrianism. In the eastern provinces, Buddhism was also widespread, the result of large-scale missionary activity. Jews, living in Babylon since their exile under Nebuchadnezzar, began to move eastward, establishing communities along the great trade and caravan routes of Mesopotamia via Iran to Afghanistan and Central Asia.

### Manichaeanism

During the reign of Shapur I, a new religion was founded by a Persian aristocrat from southern Babylonia named Mani. He came from the environment of a Jewish sect, strongly influenced by Christian, Gnostic, and Buddhist thought. When he was twelve years old and, again, when he was twenty-four, Mani saw visions of an angel making him the prophet of a new religion. He went to India to carry his message and was profound-ly influenced by Buddhism. He considered himself the final prophet in a series that included Zoroaster, Buddha, and Jesus. Mani preached a religion that postulated two com-peting principles of good (light, God, the spir-itual human soul) and evil (darkness, the devil, the material human body). He con-demned the existing world as sinful and doomed, and divided society into two classes, the *elect* and the *auditors*. The elect were ascetic, celibate vegetarians who drank no wine and did no work other than preaching. They expected to attain the realm of light after death. The lower and more numerous auditors were normal people, allowed to marry. They were expected to serve the elect in the present life, in the hope of being reborn in the higher class. Protected by Shapur I, Mani preached all over Persia and sent mis-

Part of a sixth-century
tapestry on which Khosrow I
is portrayed. He is sitting
on his throne, watching his
armies fight the enemy
forces.

1073

sionaries to the Roman Empire, provoking backlash among Zoroastrians and Christians alike. The authorities saw great danger for the existing system in Mani's fast-growing movement. Under Shapur's successor Bahram I (who reigned from 274 to 277), Mani was arrested as a heretic. He either died in prison or was killed. His religion was fiercely persecuted by Persian and Roman emperors, yet a century later, it had spread across both empires, North Africa, and, via the Silk Route, to China.

### The Kings

The successors of Shapur I were all mediocre figures until Ormazd ascended the throne in 302. He governed with extraordinary energy, gaining great popularity with the common people for his establishment of special courts

Persian gold coin with the head of Ardashir II

Silver bowl with a portrait of Khosrow I

that could protect them against the abuse of power. Ahura Mazda fell in battle against Arab Bedouins. The royal court elevated Shapur's still-unborn son to king. Confident that the child would be a boy, the court named him Shapur II even before he was born and placed the crown on his mother's abdomen. Shapur II ruled from 309 to 379, the longest reign in Persian history. The Roman Emperor Julian sent an expedition against him in 363, which ended in Julian's death. Shapur II recaptured all the territory taken by Rome, including much of Syria and Mesopotamia, with their large Christian populations. When he died, Persia stood at the apex of its power.

The Zoroastrian Yazdegerd I, who reigned from 399 to 420, permitted those Christians to worship at first, then persecuted them. His

1074

## The Legend of Sassan and Ardashir

Nothing is known for certain about Sassan, the father of Ardashir and the man after whom the Sassanid dynasty was named. In the seventh century the *Book of the Heroic Deeds of Ardashir*, was composed by a Persian priest, and is said to have served as a primary source for the poet Firdawsī.

It offers the following legend. After the death of Al-Iskander (Alexander), Iran was divided into 240 principalities. Ardavan (Artabanus), who had no sons, ruled over Ispahan, Fars (Persia), and the neighboring provinces. Sassan was a shepherd in the service of Papak, a nobleman in Fars. Papak did not know that Sassan belonged to the dynasty of Darius, the last Persian king. One night in a dream, Papak saw the sun shining on the head of Sassan and illuminating everything in the world. In another dream, he saw Sassan sitting on a white elephant while all the people in the country knelt before him. In a third dream, he saw the three holy fires of Aturfarnbag, Gusnap, and Burzin-mihr flame up in the house of Sassan and illuminate the whole world.

Papak called wise men and soothsayers together to interpret the dream. They said to him: "The man whom thou hast seen in thy dreams, or one of his successors, shall become the leader of the world. The sun and the white elephant represent might, power, and conquest. The fire Aturfarnbag represents the priests and religious scholars, the fire Gusnap the warriors, and the fire Burzinmihr the farmers. The rule over everything in the world shall be held by him or one of his sons."

Then Papak called for Sassan and asked him to which family he actually belonged. When he had promised that no penalty would befall Sassan from his answer, he heard the shepherd's secret: He was a descendant of Darius. Papak had Sassan dress at once in the robes of a courtier and gave him his own daughter as a wife. She soon became pregnant and gave birth to Ardashir. When Papak saw the boy, he understood that his dreams would come true.

Relief from Taqī-Bustān, depicting a deer hunt

He raised Ardashir as his own son. The young prince became a great horseman and archer, skilled, as well, in all the sciences. His fame spread throughout Fars. When he turned fifteen, he was summoned to the palace by Prince Ardavan. Together with the princes and the sons of other noblemen, young Ardashir went hunting every day.

One day the hunting party happened on an *onager* (a wild donkey). The oldest son of Ardavan galloped after it, but Ardashir shot it down with a single arrow. When Ardavan arrived, he marveled at the powerful shot, which his own son claimed was his. Ardashir called the prince a liar and challenged him to a contest of skill, but Ardavan erupted in anger and had Ardashir locked up in the stalls as a groom. With the aid of a slave, Ardashir managed to escape. He gathered an army, conquered Ardavan and his sons, and ascended the throne as the new ruler.

Gold coin from
the reign of Ardashir,
depicting his portrait

1075

Relief in the ruins of Naksh-i-Rustam, on which a fight between two horsemen is depicted. The central character is probably Ormuz II.

son, Bahram V, took the persecution a step further, declaring war on Rome as soon as he was crowned. The Romans defeated him two years later. The 422 treaty ending the war allowed for joint religious tolerance between Zoroastrians and Christians.

### Nestorianism

In 424, the eastern church formally separated from the western at the Council of Dad-Ishu. The importance of Christianity steadily increased in the Persian Empire over the fifth century. Most Christians were followers of the Nestorian Church, founded by the Syrian prelate Nestorius. The patriarch of Constantinople from 428 to 431, he taught that humanity and divinity existed in Jesus as distinct natures, not unified into a single personality. The doctrine was declared heretical in 431 and he was banished. By 483, Nestorianism had regained its influence and was proclaimed the official doctrine of Persian Christianity.

In the same year, the Ephthalites, called the "White Huns," defeated the Persian king Firuz II. They received tribute from the Persians until the next Sassanid king, Kavadh

I, took over. An advocate of the philosophy of the Zoroastrian high priest, Mazdak, he was deposed by his orthodox Christian brother Zamasp in 498. Three years later, Kavadh, allied with the Ephthalites, was reinstated. He battled Rome over the next two decades, gradually changing his mind about Mazdak. In 523, he authorized Mazdak's supporters massacred.

In 531, Kavadh's son, Khosrow I, succeeded him. Suspecting his brothers of conspiring to overthrow him, he had them and all their sons but one killed. Greatest of the Sassanid kings, he defeated the Byzantine emperor Justinian I in a series of wars (531–532, 540–545, 571–576), extending Persian authority west to the Black Sea, east to the Indus River, and into Central Asia. He was only defeated in 576, by Byzantine Emperor Justin II at Melitene (Turkey). He reorganized the administration of the government and the tax system, supported poor orphans out of the imperial treasury, and built dikes and canals to supply dry cities with drinking water. He created a professional army and ordered unmarried people to marry to beget recruits for it. Making Zoroastrianism once again the

Silver plate
with a depiction of a
leopard standing in a field
of lotus flowers

official religion, he drew philosophers from India and Greece to his palace. His reign led to a golden age of Persian literature. Khosrow himself, given the epithet *Anushirvan* (one who has a soul), figured in many legends.

Khosrow II, called *Parvez* (victorious), the grandson of Khosrow I, reigned from 590 to 628. Because its emperor Mauricius helped him attain the throne, he returned much of the land taken by his grandfather to Byzantium. But when Mauricius was murdered in 602, Khosrow II began a war against the Byzantine Empire that lasted the rest of his reign. He reconquered the territories restored in 592. In 613, he inflicted a great defeat on the Byzantines at Antioch, regaining Syria. The next year the Persians occupied

Remnants of the Temple of the Fire in the valley of Naksh-i-Rustam

Jerusalem, finally taking what was considered the holiest of objects, the reliquary of the cross, triumphantly home to their capital Ctesiphon. New expeditions during those years brought the Persian armies deep into Asia Minor and Egypt. By 616, Khosrow II had conquered almost all of southwestern Asia, including Palestine and Egypt. A year later, he reached Chalcedon, the old seaport across the Bosporus from Constantinople. Intrigues against him arose in Persia. Further expansion was prevented by the Byzantine emperor Heraclius. In 622, he began his great offensive with a foray into Armenia. A Persian attack on Constantinople failed. In 627, Heraclius reached the heart of the Persian Empire from Armenia, defeating Khosrow at the ruins of ancient Nineveh and returning triumphantly to the west, bearing the holy cross. The emperor was deposed and murdered by his son, Kavadh II (who reigned in 628).

The final Sassanid king was Yazdegerd III. In his reign (between 632 and 641), the Arabs seized Persia and instituted Islam as the state religion, making Persia part of their caliphate.

### Hunting and Chivalry

Originally of Scythian descent, the Parthian people wore clothing similar to that of the Medians. They spoke a language adapted from the Aryans (people who spoke an Indo-European dialect and migrated into northern India). Parthians were excellent horsemen and archers, often shooting arrows at the enemy while pretending to flee. (The phrase *a Parthian shot* has its origin in this practice, often transliterated to a *parting shot*.)

Persian sagas portray ideals of physical strength and skill reminiscent of western tales of chivalry. Hunting was the great preoccupation of the Persian court, since the desertlike area between the Tigris and Euphrates swarmed with wild animals. Princesses and the daughters of important magnates considered it a great honor to accompany the hunters on their forays, often ending up in the king's harem. Beautiful reliefs of worked sil-

Shapur II during a hunting party, depicted on a gold dish from the fourth century AD

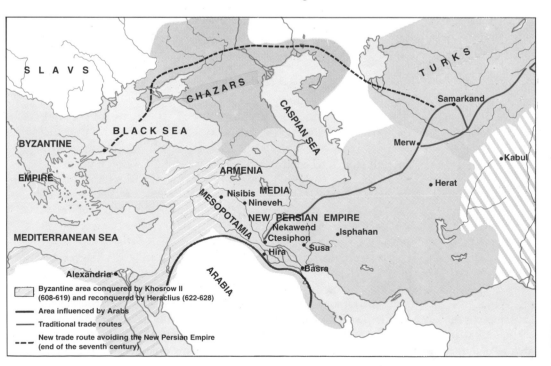

Map of the New Persian Empire in the seventh century

Miniature from
the Persian *Shah-nama*
(*Book of Kings*).
This is an illustration of the
poem about the hero
Rostam, who fights the white
devil Mazandaran.

ver have been recovered that depict these hunts, when noblemen drove game toward the king to be shot.

After a tiring day riding through the desert, the hunters would rest beside small fires in shelters along a river and tell stories to each other, often about the great Ardashir and the instructions he gave his son: "A state cannot live without religion, the destiny of a king depends on his administrators."

Despite their passion for the rough pleasures of hunting, the Persians were renowned for their manners. Respect for propriety was to them the highest law. One of their stories was about a noble prince who was sternly punished by his father, just for arriving late at a party. Even in Constantinople people knew about Persian refinement.

## Poetry

The Persians possessed an extensive store of poetry, which was enjoyed among their neighbors as well. The Arabs appreciated the romantic sensitivity of the writers. Persian influence was evident into the Middle Ages, with the poetry of the culture only reaching its full flowering around the year 1000. It was at that time that Firdawsī (also called Abū ol-Qāsem Mansūr) wrote his *Shah-nama* (*Book of Kings*).

Firdawsī was born in a village near Tus at the border of Turkestan. His father, a prosperous farmer, was able to give him a good education. Young Firdawsī learned several eastern languages, which enabled him to read the old historical texts. He soon became renowned for his epic verses. The governor of

Persian silver jar
from the seventh century,
decorated with two lions

1079

Tus, a great admirer of his poetry, put him in contact with Mahmud, a minor king of Ghazni in the eastern part of Afghanistan. Mahmud promised Firdawsī a piece of gold for every rhyming *distich* (paired lines of verse regarded as a unit) if he would write an epic poem about the adventures of the old

Silk weaving from Persia, made in the seventh century

Persian kings. The poet agreed to the proposition and spent the rest of his life composing the *Shah-nama*. Firdawsī died in Tus at eighty years of age, lonely and bitter, after sending the money back. Mahmud had betrayed him, sending the agreed number of coins in silver rather than gold.

The *Shah-nama* has been compared, justifiably, with the epic poems of Homer. It possesses the same cultural, aesthetic, and historical value, but while Homer's works, the *Iliad* and the *Odyssey*, take place within a single generation, the *Shah-nama* covers the history of Persia before the Arab conquest. It even begins with a mythological summary of creation. This is followed by the histories of the Persian kings. Their heroic deeds are fantastic: they fight with armies of elephants and horses, they describe terrifying enemies, they annihilate the neighboring Turanians who continually harass the Persians. Most of the episodes, like the tale of Khosru and Sirin, concern kings.

Alexander the Great also plays a leading role in the *Shah-nama*. As Al-Iskander, the son of Philip II and a woman from "Rumiras" (easily read here as Romanus or Roman), he enjoyed amazing adventures. Firdawsī describes his love for his mother, and the wise advice of Aristatalis (Aristotle), "a respected man among the Rum, very intelligent, cautious, and ambitious." Both of them, mother and teacher, stood at the deathbed of the great Al-Iskander, Firdawsī assures us. This is followed by a long story concerning a disagreement about his burial place. Finally, "a wise man from the province" spoke: "Why do you store the body of Alexander for so long? His land is Iskenderich (Alexandria), which he created while still alive." Together, the legends concerning Al-Iskander amount to a tenth of the whole *Shah-nama*; it is no wonder that Alexander, of all the conquerors, made the greatest impression on the East.

Firdawsī's tales are vivid with detail. Alexander goes west to where the sea begins and sees people "of whom only the teeth are white." He visits places where the people have only one leg. He makes his way into the city of the Amazons to find out how they reproduce. He treks over mountain chains that reach the sky. He goes to Msir (Egypt) and India, where he admires the Brahmans for their wisdom. In the East, he encounters the monsters Gog and Magog and builds a wall that nothing and no one can penetrate. The *Shah-nama* ends with the murder of the last Persian King, Yazdegerd, who suffered defeat at the hands of Caliph Ali's Arab troops. Firdawsī himself, a pious Muslim, had great admiration for Ali and his armies, so he ends his epic in this way: "That he may maintain understanding, knowledge, and nobility, that he may be the light of the Persians and Arabs. I leave this great poem, which consists of six times ten thousand couplets, behind for him. It shall be my glory; I shall not die. My name shall be immortal. I have explained how to write well. The wise men shall bless my memory when I no longer exist . . . I send one thousand and one blessings and praises to the prophet chosen by God, and to the members of his family, out of respect for the religion."

The archangel Gabriel appears unto the prophet Muhammad. Detail of a fifteenth-century miniature

# Muhammad

*Creator of a World Religion*

Throughout the Roman and Byzantine periods and until the beginning of the seventh century AD, the Arabian Peninsula remained on the periphery of the political, urban, and religious developments in the eastern part of the Mediterranean and North Africa. With the exception of the Nabatean Kingdom (with its capital at Petra in today's Jordan) and small Byzantine vassal princedoms on the borders between what are today Syria and Arabia, the peninsula, mostly desert, attracted little attention from the imperial powers, from Alexander the Great to the Byzantine emperors. Most of the population of the peninsula were pagan, socially fragmented into tribes, relying on a pastoral economy. Although there were urban communities in the western edge of the peninsula, called al-Hijaz, the cities of Mecca and Medina were not comparable to the major Middle Eastern cities of the time. They were far smaller than the imperial seat of Constantinople and such other cities as Damascus.

This, however, does not characterize the life of the Arabians, because centuries before the development of Islam, the inhabitants of the peninsula were in close contact with the imperial centers in Syria and Mesopotamia. Waves of migrant people moved north and

A camel driver and his family, depicted on a stele from the south of Arabia. The relief dates from the time before Islam.

northeast and settled in Syria and Mesopotamia, integrating with the local populations. The interior was inhabited by nomadic tribes called Arabs. They had to endure the harsh weather, the barren land, and the scarcity of water, as they moved from one oasis to another with their herds.

## The Bedouin

The hordes of Bedouins who trekked through the desert were warlike travelers whom few dared take lightly. Although real desert dwellers are able to eke out a sustenance from their barren environment, they never find enough food or water to enable them to live sedentary lives. By definition, therefore, desert dwellers like the Bedouin people of the Arabian Peninsula are essentially nomads. Riding their slow camels, they move from oasis to oasis, seeking out the sparse meadows found in some of the *wadis* (oases). They subsist on the milk of their mounts, occasional meat from their herds of sheep and goats, and figs and dates from the oasis palms. They trade for rice, other food items, and the few essentials they use. Their lifestyle has altered little over the centuries.

In a desert that knew no political borders, authority covered not regions, but people. The Bedouin owned no land. They formed families and tribes that commanded their loyalty, rather than territory. The only leader they recognized was the elder they called the sheik. Sometimes he was chosen, sometimes he came from some prominent family. His task was not to rule over the tribe; the individualistic desert dwellers would not have tolerated that. His job was to find good solutions to the conflicts endemic among the proud Bedouin. All too often, small problems would escalate into internecine feuds involving increasing numbers of people. When entire tribes played a role in the mutual violence, the result was sometimes war lasting for years. The history of Arabia is a tale of complicated clashes, often taking the form of blood vendettas.

Deeds of war among the Bedouins were not forgotten. Each tribe had its own poet who recorded the deeds of its warriors in the form of verse, an oral history. The tribal wars were the basis of epic poems. The recurring bloodbaths gave birth to a whole range of literature. To this very day, poetry is an important form of artistic expression among the Arabic-speaking people. Metrical styles developed in the sixth century AD remained in use until modern times, when new free forms replaced them.

## The City

Arabia knew only a few cities in the west and south of the peninsula. However, these cities (Mecca, Yathrib, Saria) never attained the size and magnitude of other cities in Syria and Anatolia. Almost none survived because of the use of mud brick in construction. An oasis would sometimes become a center of cultural outreach when a particular dynasty put an end to the anarchy normally

Muhammad (who has covered his face)
with a group of his followers. Page from a book
about the prophet's life, probably produced
in the sixteenth century

reigning in the desert. Some oases even
became the centers of small empires, but
oasis towns in general remained on the
fringes of society. Their nomadic neighbors
were too quarrelsome to accept the establishment of political unity: Arabia remained in
political chaos. Any unity that existed was
fostered by religion. The Arabs revered an
array of gods and spirits with one common
point: most Arabs recognized the religious
importance of the temple called the *Kaaba*
(the cube). This housed figurines represent-
ing various gods that were worshiped by the
tribes. It functioned as a sort of religious center. The Bedouin traveled to it to honor their
gods. Nothing is known about the origin of
the Kaaba. The temple just stood there, built
in the neat square shape from which it got its
name.

The caravan city of Mecca grew around

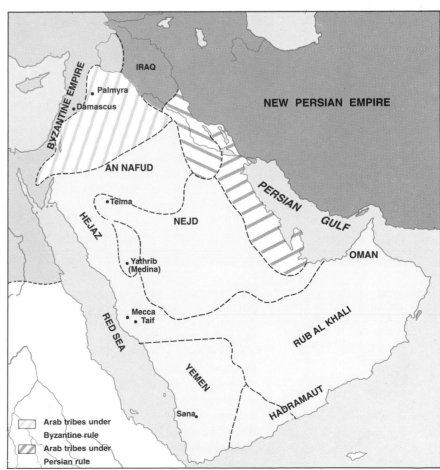

Arabia
before Islam

this holy spot. Trade and pilgrimages had brought into being the greatest concentration of people in all Arabia. Nonetheless, Mecca was anything but impressive. The average Byzantine visitor must have found it quite provincial. However, for Arabia, the city was a window on the world. In its streets, there

Muhammad is visited by a group of aristocrats from Medina, who ask him to settle in their city. Persian miniature from the fifteenth century

was something of a cosmopolitan atmosphere. There was a Jewish neighborhood, a few Christians, and traders from the Mediterranean. The management of Mecca was in the hands of a group of wealthy families also involved in commercial matters.

Farther to the east lay Medina (literally meaning "the city"). It formed the center of an oasis whose wells promised rich harvests. But Medina was notable for more than its water resources. Its population was, to a great extent, Jewish. It is assumed that immi-

grants from Palestine had won over the original inhabitants to their beliefs, allowing Medina to become an isolated Jewish fortress.

Christians and Jews, traders and pilgrims, the region of Arabia that held Mecca and Medina was particularly suited to the birth of new ways of thinking. Its society differed radically from that of the desert and most of the oases. In 570, the prophet Muhammad was born in Mecca. He came from an important family, one that held a key position in the administration of the Kaaba.

## Muhammad's Youth

Muhammad's father had died three months before the birth of his son. As an adult, the prophet would remember only the Bedouin wet nurse from his earliest youth, who had cared for him in the desert for two years. He was already a sturdy little boy when the wet nurse returned him to his mother, but his mother did not want him. "Take the child with you again, and return to the desert, so that he does not become ill from the unhealthy air of Mecca," she was to have said in an excess of concern. Muhammad spent another three years in the tents and the traditions of the Bedouin. They acquainted him with their ways of thinking, their values, and the language of their poetry. "I am an Arab from head to toe," Muhammad would say later. "I come from the Quaraysh of Mecca, and speak the language of the Beni Assas [the tribe of his wet nurse]."

It was not until his fifth year that Muhammad went to the house of his mother in Mecca, but she died eight months later, and Muhammad was sent to live with his grandfather. Three years after that, the grandfather died. The then nine-year-old Muhammad went to the home of his uncle, Abu Talib. (In that light, it is interesting to note how the Koran demands care for people without parents.) Muhammad's family was not rich. His father had only left him three camels and a slave, and his uncle was not particularly well-off. He owned a small flock of sheep and goats that Muhammad tended on the dry plains around Mecca. "There has never been a prophet who has not been a shepherd," Muhammad would later say.

## From Camel Driver to Trader

Muhammad's uncle, Abu Talib, was not concerned with agriculture alone. Like most residents of Mecca, he was active in trade. The merchants pooled their resources to send caravans across the desert to Damascus in Syria and to Egypt. When Abu Talib could no longer support his nephew, he advised him to

Illustration from
an Arabian manuscript
depicting the city
of Medina

هذا مدينة منور

find a job with the caravans sent out by the rich widow Khadijah; Muhammad entered her employ. Although she was fifteen years older than him, they married that same year.

At the age of twenty-five, Muhammad had a wife, money, and a business. He could dedicate himself to the pleasant life of a stay-at-home merchant. His caravans trekked through Arabia, bringing him and his wife new riches. Yet this was evidently not a marriage-for-money. Years later, Muhammad would still tell his friends that he never loved anyone more than he loved Khadijah.

Muhammad may have always been a mystic. He knew the traditions of the Bedouin and was familiar with the countless beliefs of Mecca. He had experienced the awe-inspiring loneliness of the desert. According to tradition, around his fortieth year he began to have visions. One of them was of a meeting with the archangel Gabriel, retold here.

Muhammad was sitting in meditation in the hills near Mecca when suddenly the angel Gabriel appeared before him. The angel said to him: "Repeat after me, in the name of God, the creator who created man from coagulated blood, repeat after me: because your God is full of goodness; it is he who has taught us, it is he who has taught us what we did not know. Man is indeed arrogant that he may obtain riches. If we must

A reliquary
that is said to
contain one of
Muhammad's
teeth

thank our God for all we have, what does thou think, then, of those who fail to pray to God's servant? Have they listened well? Hast thou not seen how they refuse to pay attention to the truth? How can this be! They know not that God sees all things! Verily, if they shall fail to better themselves we shall pull them away by the locks of hair on their foreheads. The liars and the sinners, by the

epileptic Jewish youth who came from Medina was known to walk around softly humming prophecies through his teeth. This humming, incidentally, was the standard way of prophesying. Arabia knew many kahins who regularly went into trances. The sound they brought forth was called *sach*, the cooing of doves.

The people around Muhammad were not particularly shocked then, by his revelations. Only the prophet himself experienced spiritual difficulties. He wanted to be sure that his visions really came from God. If a *jinn* (a spirit) had taken possession of him, and such things were thought possible at any time, then he had become a magician and not a prophet. Meanwhile, the revelations continued: sometimes an angel appeared, sometimes the holy message came through in other ways. Muhammad complained: "Sometimes it comes to me in the sound of a clock, and the most painful for me is that I then lose it, and must remember what was said. At times it comes to me as a man who comes to talk to me, and then I remember his words."

The revelations were exhausting. It is said that when Muhammad heard them, he sometimes perspired heavily even on the coldest days. It is said that the prophet even avoided foods with garlic, so as not to offend the angel. The Koran says in sura (chapter) 20: "We have caused a Koran to descend in the Arabian language . . . do not rush to repeat it as long as the revelation is not complete. Say, instead: 'God, increase my knowledge.'"

Map of Mecca on which the sanctuaries are marked. In the right upper corner the Kaaba (the most holy Muslim sanctuary in Mecca) can be seen. Illustration from an Arabian manuscript

locks of hair on their foreheads. Let them call their fellow men! We shall call upon the powers of hell. No, do not humble yourselves. Praise and approach your God."

**From Tradesman to Prophet**

From that point on, Muhammad considered himself a prophet. He repeated Gabriel's words to his wife. With the encouragement of Khadijah, he delved deeper into spiritual concerns. Visions and revelations were not considered unusual in Arabia, especially in the society of Mecca, where people were readily open to religious experience.

In Muhammad's time, for example, an

# Islam

## The Birth of a New World Religion

Many of Muhammad's desert contemporaries venerated the moon and stars and many idols at the Kaaba, the traditional shrine in Mecca. They saw heaven and earth populated by innumerable gods, headed by the one they called Allah (Arabic for "God"). What Muhammad learned from the angel Gabriel was that there was but one God, Allah, creator of all that existed, good and just, demanding honor from all mortals. He rewarded the devout and punished the wicked. Muhammad believed people not only said useless prayers when they directed them toward nonexistent gods, they insulted Allah, for which they would be punished. Disputing the Bedouin conviction, he said that Allah was far more than a tribal god, but was universal, the only God. Muhammad

1087

Muhammad, his daughter Fatima, his son-in-law Ali, and some of his cousins. Arabian miniature painting from the fifteenth century

considered the Yahweh of the Jews and the God of the Christians simply other names for the same god, Allah. He forbid idolatry, even as practiced by his own tribe, the Quraysh.

The creed of Islam, formulated by Muhammad, is stated in a single phrase: There is no God but Allah, and Muhammad is his prophet. Followers of Islam (which means submitting [to the will of God]) are called Muslims (the Arabic word for "those who submit"). They revere Muhammad as the greatest of the prophets but also honor Noah, Abraham (common ancestor of Jews and Arabs), and Moses, who gave the Hebrews their law five centuries after Abraham first spoke to them of Yahweh. Jesus is likewise seen as a prophet, but regarded as human, not divine.

By the time of Jesus, the Jewish Bible had been divided into sections called the Law, the Prophets, and the Psalms, the tale of heroic deeds, the chronicles of history, and the lessons of the writings. Texts of these have been found in the Dead Sea Scrolls, the work of many people. The holy writ of Islam, the Koran, in contrast, is said to be the work of the uneducated Muhammad alone. Over a span of twenty-two years its 78,000

words were revealed to him and recorded by a scribe. Companion to it in guiding the daily life of Muslims is the Hadith (Story), which details incidents in Muhammad's life, as well as his particular preferences and maxims.

According to Islamic tradition, Allah had caused 104 books to descend from the heavens to the earth to present truth to mankind. Even the first human being, Adam, had received ten books. Other Old Testament figures had received their share: Seth had been given fifty, Enoch thirty, Abraham ten, and Moses one. However, over the course of time, nearly all of those books had been lost. Only the one given to Moses, called the Pentateuch, and the last three books, the psalms of David, the gospel of Jesus, and the Koran, given to Muhammad himself, had been saved. They contained the holy truth. Only the Koran, according to Muhammad, was entirely reliable. He added to its verses throughout his life as new revelations came to him. (These were organized after his death into 114 chapters called suras.) The other scriptures, differing considerably from the teachings of the Koran, were in his view distorted by the Jews and the Christians who had lost their pure monotheism. The greatest distortion, he said, was the claim of the Christians that God had a son. This was unthinkable to Muhammad, an assault on the majesty of Allah.

## The Five Pillars of Islam

The basic tenets of Islam, as written in the Koran, state: "We believe in God and in that which has been sent down on us and . . . on Abraham, Ishmael, Isaac, and Jacob, and their progeny, and that which was given to Moses and Jesus and the Prophets by their Lord; we make no distinction among any of them and to Him we submit." (Sura II, 136)

"True piety is this: to believe in God, and the Last Day, the angels, the Book [the Koran], and the Prophets; to give of one's substance, however cherished, to kinsmen and orphans, the needy, the traveler, beggars, and to free the slave; to perform the prayer; to pay the alms. And they who fulfill their covenant . . . these are the truly god-fearing." (Sura II, 177)

The Koran establishes five obligations for the faithful. The first is acceptance of the basic creed that Allah is the only god and that Muhammad is his prophet. With this comes an obligation to pray. *Salah* (ritual prayer) is to be performed, facing Mecca, five times daily, at dawn, noon, late afternoon, sunset, and after dark. Before the prayers, ablutions with water (or sand) are to be performed. *Du'a* (private prayer) can be done any time.

The Koran insists that belief be put into practice, in the form of good deeds and the giving of alms to the poor. This is the third requirement. The good deeds are done to honor Allah, who wants to see the belief of his servants confirmed. Muhammad said, according to the Hadith, "A man's true wealth hereafter is the good he does in this world to his fellowmen."

The fourth obligation is to fast during the month of Ramadan, and the fifth is to make at least one *hajj* (pilgrimage) to Mecca in one's lifetime.

Muhammad flees to Medina with some of his followers. Miniature painting from an Arabian manuscript probably dating from the fifteenth century

Muhammad strips the Kaaba (the most holy Muslim sanctuary in Mecca) of all idols. Only the black stone is left in its place.

1090

Much of the Koran employs vivid and colorful language. On the Day of Resurrection, the dead rise to be judged. The righteous cross a bridge to eternal bliss in lush gardens of delight. There, fountains spout wine (forbidden to mortals while they live). There will be laden tables, soft beds, and five hundred *houris* (young virgins) to grant caresses to each blessed soul. Even wives will respect these houris; at the right hand of God there could be no jealousy. The damned are thrown into an abyss to wear "garments of fire" that burn their skin. It grows back, only to be repeatedly destroyed. In an atmosphere of decay, they drink pus and boiling liquids.

The Koran also deals with the building of human community by godly regulation. Muhammad prescribed rules of behavior to correct the social evils of his time, one of which was the abuse of alcohol. He saw it as a duty of the believer to protect widows and orphans, allowing polygamy as a means of shelter for women where men died young. He took ten wives himself after his first one died, before the Koranic number was limited to four. Divorce was a matter of repeating, "Thou art dismissed"; both wife and husband had property rights.

## The First Believers

Muhammad had few followers at first. They included his wife, Khadijah, the house slave, Said, and his cousin Ali, a son of Abu Talib. His first convert outside his family was the merchant, Abū Bakr. Like Muhammad, he despaired of the idolatry and superstition that reigned in Mecca.

One of Muhammad's postulates was that believers could not be slaves, so attempts had to be made to buy the freedom of converted slaves. Abū Bakr spent four thousand silver coins in doing so, undoubtedly enhancing the prophet's popularity among the slaves.

Muhammad also attracted the attention of the wealthy. Three rich merchants, Talha, Abderrahman, and Othman converted, giving their fortunes to the young religion. The black slave Bilal converted at about the same time. Noted for the quality of his voice, he would become the first *muezzin* (announcer of the hour of prayer) to call the faithful to worship.

## The Kaaba (House of God)

The cubic building called the Kaaba (Arabic for cube) housed more than 300 statues. It was considered holy by most of the Arabians. They came to Mecca to worship at it from all over the peninsula. Muhammad and his followers, in light of his teaching against idolatry and his concept of the one-

ness of God, removed the statues from the Kaaba with the exception of a black stone. The stone became the focal point of the Kaaba, as it was believed to have been sent by God from heaven.

A black stone had also been the central

point of a holy place built by Ismael and his father Abraham on the special instructions of Allah. When his first wife, Sarah, was expecting the baby Isaac, Abraham sent his second wife, Hagar, into the desert with their son Ismael. The Old Testament describes Yahweh saving both their lives and Ismael becoming the tribal leader of the Arabs. The Koran specifies that Allah let Ismael and Hagar discover a well at Zemzem, providing

A reconstruction of Muhammad's room in Medina, as shown in the Topkapi Museum in Istanbul

them water to live in that area. The holy place was erected in gratitude.

Muhammad had made himself unpopular with the upper classes in Mecca with his objections to traditional idol worship and his advocacy of the worth of each individual.

Miniature from a fourteenth-century manuscript in which Muhammad is depicted in heaven

His ideas contradicted the accepted religious concepts, but, even more, the prophet was not only sacrilegious, he was bad for business. Quraysh men who sold food, water, and robes for ritual use around the Kaaba lost money as Muhammad won converts. The indifference of many citizens toward him turned to antipathy and persecution. Some Muslims fled across the Red Sea to Ethiopia. Muhammad and his followers withdrew to the house of Abu Talib on the outskirts of Mecca. They stayed there, exiled, afraid to leave the house, for three years. The town authorities stoned and beat the converts when they saw them. During this difficult time, Khadijah and Abu Talib died.

## The Hegira, September 20, 622

Eventually the situation became unbearable. Muhammad, already told of plots against him, had a vision that told him to leave for Yathrib, 250 miles (400 kilometers) north of hostile Mecca. On September 20, 622, he and a hundred of his disciples departed. The date of that *hegira* (flight) is used as the first day of the Muslim calendar. It was Monday when they arrived in Koba, an outlying town, where they waited for popular reaction. They entered the city on Friday. Just outside its gates, Muhammad stepped down to pray. A mosque would later be built on the spot and Friday would become the Muslim Sabbath. Yathrib was renamed Madinat al-Nabi (the city of the prophet) or Medina.

## Al-Medina, Cradle of Islam

Medina was a favorable breeding ground for Muhammad's teachings. The Jewish tribes who made up a large section of the population there were familiar with monotheism. The prophet was welcomed with cheers. "Step down, Prophet, and stay among us," called the multitudes, "we have room for you, and weapons with which to defend you." Muhammad replied that he would leave his decision to his camel. The animal stood by a courtyard where a few palm trees grew. It is said that Muhammad stayed and built the first mosque there.

Within ten years, the fugitive prophet was spiritual leader and head of state. He quickly won followers, who were in the majority and actually ruled the city. Only the Jews rejected his teachings and his politics. The Meccans, meanwhile, did not leave their runaway son alone, repeatedly battling with Medina.

The Jews, not interested in war, remained impartial at best. Muhammad then took measures against them, banning a number of Jews from the city, killing others, and forcing the rest into subservient positions. After seizing Jewish possessions around the city, Muhammad devised a law that Muslims since have applied for centuries to people of other religions. The Jews could continue to exercise their beliefs under official protection, but they had to pay a special tax to do so.

As battles with Mecca continued, the people of Medina routinely defeated the Meccans, although once they were forced back to their city gates. Muhammad himself fought and was noted for both bravery and strategy. He cut off Mecca's caravan routes,

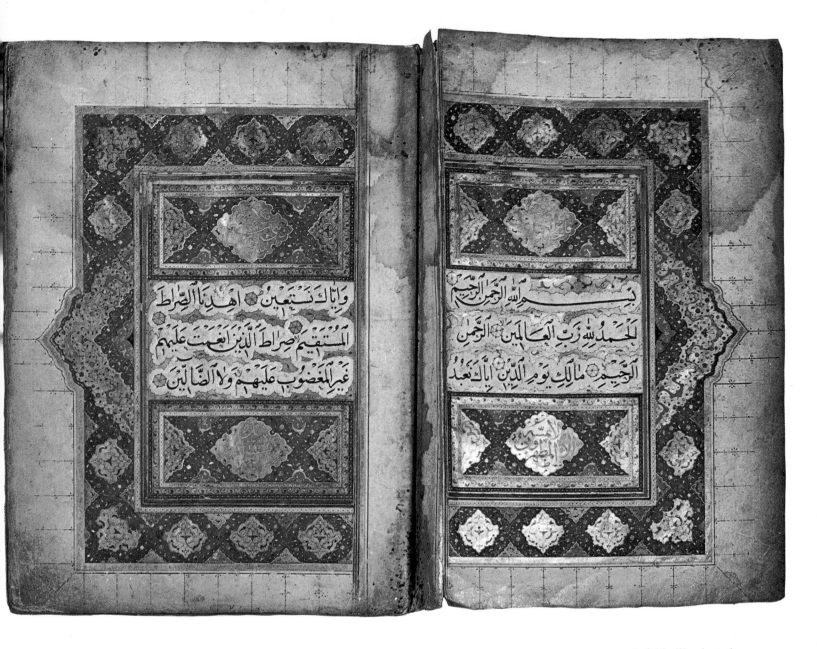

undermining its economy. In 624, he led 300 Muslims against a much larger force of Meccans. His victory was taken as a sign of Allah's approval. By 628, Mecca was ready to sign a ten-year truce giving Muslims free access to the Kaaba.

The next year, the first pilgrimage to Mecca was held, resulting in thousands of conversions, even among the urban elite. At the beginning of 630, Muhammad entered Mecca with 10,000 followers. The city offered little resistance. He circled the Kaaba by camel seven times, ordered the idols destroyed, and rededicated the building to Allah.

Muhammad treated the city of his birth with care. He made it possible for his erstwhile enemies to work for him, giving them honorable positions and allowing them to share in the spoils of war. His victories had an impact on the beliefs of those who were skeptical about his religious message, as they began to be viewed as the work of the One God. It seemed advantageous to worship Allah.

## Ummah

A wave of conversions occurred among the Bedouin. Representatives of numerous tribes came to offer their submission to Muhammad, both spiritually and politically. Muhammad became a theocrat, ruling a huge population, body and soul. He had united the disparate, chronically feuding Arabs of the desert into a brotherhood called the ummah. His control was rooted in the theological conviction of his supporters. His sphere of influence was limited only by the forts that the Byzantines and the Persians had built on the edge of the desert.

Gradually, Muhammad began treating his opponents with less tolerance. In 631, he formally announced the persecution of the remaining nonbelievers. At the conclusion of the holy period (when differences were traditionally put aside), he said they

1093

would be declared outlaws, no longer permitted freedom to worship near the Kaaba. This threat was sufficient to bring him more converts. A year later, few Arabs had failed to embrace the religion of Muhammad, at least outwardly.

Until his last years, the prophet lived in poverty, shaking the ever-present lice from his blankets himself and saddling his own camel. As a poor Arab, he lived on dates and curdled milk.

Nonetheless, he continued to be seen as a spiritual leader who founded a holy state dedicated to the greater glory of Allah, not himself. The prophet made no effort to take advantage of his followers. He was satisfied with a low tax, enough to cover the costs of his administration. He carried out that administration in moderate fashion, acting in the manner of a great sheik, preventing conflicts within his own tribe. In general, his administration appears to have been successful. No rebellions were reported, even after his death. On the contrary, the foundation Muhammad laid proved solid. From their Arabian and Bedouin bases, his successors would conquer new continents.

In 632, Muhammad fell ill and died. The faithful spread legends concerning his death. Just before it, one said, Allah sent an angel to ask his great servant whether he wished to remain alive. Muhammad replied that he wanted whatever God wanted. His last words were: "God, forgive me and allow me to come to you in heaven."

## The Caliphs

By the time Muhammad died, he had largely outlined the guidelines of the religion he had established. His followers lived according to the principles he had revealed. People everywhere said they feared Allah, but the depth of their conviction might have been easily overestimated. To many people of that time, it was no doubt remarkable that the power of the new religion continued.

Muhammad was survived by only his beautiful daughter Fatima and her two sons, Hassan and Hussein. He had not named a successor. There had been little thought given to the inevitability of his death. Now

In a dream, Muhammad sees a ladder leading from the Kaaba to paradise, which consists of seven levels.
Muhammad arrives in the first heaven with the archangel Gabriel and the horse Borak.
This horse has a woman's face, the body of a horse, and the tail of a peacock.
Miniature painting possibly from fifteenth-century India

various parties of converts attempted to seize power. His companions finally settled on old Abū Bakr, the exile who had once left Mecca with the prophet. Declared the first *caliph* (successor), he was given the authority of Muhammad himself. Like Muhammad, he had become the leader of the faithful, spiritually and politically. He ruled the holy state.

For centuries, caliphs would rule over the Muslims. As believers, the people could have only one leader. If several people proclaimed themselves successor to the prophet, some of them, by definition, had to be false. Eventually, competing caliphs would divide Islam, each trying to prove his legality as the only descendant of Muhammad, insisting his competitors were usurpers.

There was no separation of church and state in traditional Muslim realms. A caliph is considered to have religious obligations as well as governmental. The later rulers of Baghdad, Cairo, and Córdoba, all Muslim realms, would preach each Friday in the mosques, and the caliph of Baghdad would at one point accuse the inhabitants of Damascus of having an unworthy lifestyle. In practice, however, the spiritual element of a caliphate was frequently pushed into the background as individual caliphs became

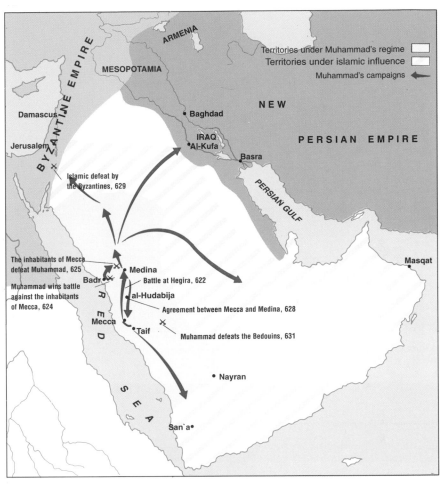

Arabia
at the time of
Muhammad

preoccupied with other issues of government.

Abū Bakr ruled only for two years. During that short time he held off the domestic enemies of Islam, consolidating Muslim authority in areas where Muhammad had not yet done so and making plans for larger enterprises. His Bedouin tribesmen began to act aggressively at the northern border against the two great powers of his time, Persia and the Eastern Roman Empire.

Near Badr, Muhammad and this troops win a battle against the inhabitants of Mecca. This fourteenth-century miniature depicts some scenes of the fight.

1095

Muhammad arrives in the seventh heaven with the archangel Gabriel and is received by a choir of angels. Miniature from the fifteenth century

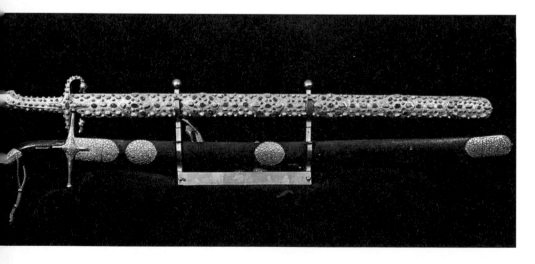

These two richly decorated sheaths contain the swords that once belonged to Muhammad.

## The *Jihad*

*Jihad*, literally meaning to make an effort (implicitly, for the sake of the cause) is popularly interpreted as "Holy War." The concept developed along with Islam itself. In the early days of the religion, the jihad took several forms. These included participating in the defense of the Muslim community, donating money or goods to that community, and overcoming the temptation to return to pagan beliefs. The term became most popular as a description of Muslim conquest, especially in the early periods of Islamic history.

Muhammad had taught that his convictions should be defended with weapons. Even in Medina, battle had become an essential part of Islam. The idea behind the jihad can be summarized as the world consisted of two areas, one belonging to Allah and the other an area of chaos. Allah's region was ruled for him by his followers. It was the task of every believer to expand Allah's territory or to diminish chaos, on both the individual and the social level.

The Bedouin, who constituted the bulk of the Muslim army at the time, had never undertaken more than an occasional marauding expedition. They had usually allowed themselves to be played against each other

Persian miniature > depicting Muhammad (with a covered face) sitting on a throne in heaven, surrounded by angels

by the Persians and the Byzantines, but now they believed they had the protection of Allah. Convinced that defeat was impossible, they threw themselves on their opponents.

This element of idealism was in many aspects particularly significant in the battle.

Muhammad hands
the double-pointed sword
of Islam
to his son-in-law Ali.

It was certainly no band of hypocritical roving bandits who came out of the desert on their camels. Caliph Abū Bakr, for example, initially refused any compensation for his activities. Later on, he reserved an annual salary of 6,000 pounds for himself, but in his will he required that all his salary be paid back after the sale of his property. Allah occupied a greater place in the heart of the Arabs than their opponents often wished to believe.

In another context, as well, the teachings of the jihad were important. In contrast to their exploits of the past, the Arabs were no longer on simple marauding expeditions. They were bent on conquest for religious purpose. Around 650, Jerusalem was conquered.

The capitulation agreement of the city has been preserved: "In the name of the merciful God: this is a contract for the people of Jerusalem. The servant of God, the leader of the faithful, the commander of the true, assures the people of Jerusalem that their lives and properties, their churches, their crosses, and everything which surrounds them to honor them, shall be spared. Their churches shall not be destroyed, changed, or confiscated, nor shall the crosses or the property of the residents. No one shall be forced to give up his religion or (in the exercise thereof) be hindered. The Jews shall live in Jerusalem and shall, just like the Christians, only be required to pay the contributions which are paid in other cities, but no one shall have to pay these taxes before he shall have brought in his harvest. If some people wish to leave and wish to take their property with them, and wish to give up their churches and crosses, then they shall receive safe passage to make it possible for them to reach a safe place."

The concept that the early Muslims had of their conquests was of an entirely different nature than any previous military campaigns, including those of Alexander of Macedonia, the Romans, the Visigoths, or the Huns. The purpose of their conquests was the establishment of a rule they believed in their hearts to be just.

Musicians and standard-bearers of an Islamic caravan returning from the pilgrimage to Mecca. Miniature from the *Makamat*, a picturesque novel from the fourteenth century, written by al-Hariri

# Jihad

## *Holy War in the Name of Allah*

In 632, when Muhammad died, international politics in the Middle East were determined, as they had been in the past, by conflicts between Persia (first under the Parthians and then the Sassanians) and the Eastern Roman (or Byzantine) Empire. Constantinople carried the torch passed to it by Rome with great conviction. The enmity between the emperor and the Persian king escalated. While Muhammad preached in Medina, the two empires were involved in a life-and-death battle. At one point, the Persians had even reached the coasts of the Bosporus Strait. Byzantine Emperor Heraclius could almost see his enemies from his palace at the capital in Constantinople. With enormous effort, his forces were able to drive the Persian troops back to their own territory.

There were no winners in these conflicts, only victims: the people who lived in the areas being fought over, the taxpayers who were drained. Ctesiphon (the Sassanian capital near what is now Baghdad) and Constantinople were just about equally balanced, their rulers equally hated by their people. Emperor Heraclius was an orthodox Christian with nothing but contempt for the Monophysical ideas of his Syrian and Egyptian subjects. (The doctrine of Monophysicism held that Jesus Christ had

Ali's followers swear him an oath of fidelity, while his double-edged sword is shown. Persian miniature from the fourteenth century

only a single nature, which was divine, not human. Orthodox Christians said he possessed both qualities.) The Persian king set out to make his subjects accept the teachings of Zarathustra, by violent means if necessary. The Persian Empire had come to a political crisis. A rebellious nobility surrounded a shaky crown, taxes were much too high, and all significant power lay in the hands of mercenaries. This was how things stood when the troops of Abū Bakr, successor to Muhammad, arrived near Syria.

## The Great Attack

"I have ten commandments to give you: Do not cheat and do not steal. Do not betray. Do not injure anyone. Kill no children, women, or old people. Burn no palm trees. Cut down no fruit trees. Do not destroy any harvests. Kill no livestock or camels, unless this shall be to obtain food for yourselves. Make offerings to the monks with shorn heads. Leave the hermits alone."

This was the uncommonly benign code of ethics Abū Bakr had given his fighters. This time the civilian population would have a pleasant impression of their invaders. After all, the mercenaries who fought the wars for those in power were used to plundering. Syrian residents were accustomed to inva-

sions and generally attempted to maintain their normal lifestyles. Now the Arabs were giving them generous opportunities to conduct business as usual, so there was no reason for the people to resist them. The Byzantine authorities saw that the heavily robed fighters from the desert could wage war better than their own disciplined troops. Within a year, Constantinople had lost whole provinces.

## Omar

Abū Bakr ruled for only two years, but was able to avoid the mistake Muhammad had made in not choosing a *caliph* (successor). Just before his death, he appointed the Muslim merchant Omar, who had joined Muhammad even before the flight to Medina.

Omar proved to be an effective and pow-erful caliph. In his first speech in the mosque of Medina, he said, "The Arabs are like a restless camel which one must force to move. On the God of the Kaaba, I swear to you that I shall lead you where you must go."

While his generals realized great successes everywhere, Omar directed strategy from Medina. He only left the capital on one occasion, when the Arabs took Jerusalem. His plan was quite successful. Attacking Persia and the Eastern Roman (or Byzantine) Empire simultaneously, his generals conquered the Byzantines in Syria and drove the Persians out of Mesopotamia. They took Damascus after a six-month occupation.

Caliph Omar proscribed six obligatory and six desirable rules of conduct for his new subjects. They were not permitted to ridicule the Koran or Muhammad, to marry Muslim women, to attempt to convert a Muslim, to

A group of camel drivers takes a rest. Miniature from the *Makamat* by al-Hariri

1101

View of the old part
of the city of Jerusalem.
In the middle is the Dome of
the Rock, the mosque
that was built during the reign
of Abd al-Malik, probably
on the very spot where
the altar of King Solomon
used to stand.

wound or to rob anyone, or to help their enemies. It was desirable that nonbelievers be recognizable by their clothing, at the very least, by wearing a yellow cloth. They were not allowed to build houses higher than those of Muslims, to ring bells (a standard way of calling Christians to worship), or to read their scriptures aloud. They could drink no wine in public and had to keep their pigs hidden from the view of Muslim believers. They were not permitted to ride horses, but could use mules or donkeys.

The Arab conquest continued without civilian rebellion. In 637, Ctesiphon, the capital of the Persian kings, fell. In 639, Arab troops marched on the town of Al-Arish, the gateway to Egypt. Two years later, the Byzantines were forced out of Alexandria. The Arabs made it known that they did not intend to leave the vanquished

area. At the suggestion of Omar, fortified towns were founded in the new territories. The conquerors of Egypt built Al-Fustat, while those of Mesopotamia built Basra and Al-Kufa. Far more than military camps, they became places where Arabian traditions and lifestyle were cultivated.

The vast store of goods seized from the conquered rulers was exploited for the new government. The great hunting parks once used by the Persian aristocracy were even partially reclaimed. The income from these properties went directly to Medina, where the caliph used it to pay his veterans.

In 644, Omar was felled by the sword of a Christian slave. He lived for a few days, able to discuss the choice of his successor with his aides. Eventually the decision was left to the council of elders. They chose Othman, another of Muhammad's original converts.

This minaret stands near the Dome of the Rock in Jerusalem. Minarets are special structures where the call to prayer takes place.

He was not particularly powerful, but this was not considered a liability because Omar had developed such a strong foundation for the empire. An additional reason for selecting Omar was the fact that he came from the old mercantile aristocracy of Mecca, which could now, via the caliph, regain its lost status.

This, indeed, happened. Othman put his peers in key positions, particularly his own clan, the Ambitious. This was not particularly popular with other groups who had been driven from power by Muhammad's old enemies. The opposition gathered around Muhammad's son-in-law Ali, who was married to the lovely Fatima, daughter of the prophet.

## The First Schism

Revolution was in the air. Many Bedouin felt that a disproportionate amount of the profits from both war and peace went to Medina. Then there were the religious disputes about the proper formulation of the Koran. Ali and Muhammad's widow, Aisha, did what they could to fan the flames.

When Othman was murdered in his own house in 656, any appearance of unity among the rebels was finished. Ali began carrying out the tasks of the caliph and met with much resistance. He felt it would be more sensible to relocate from Medina to Al-Kufa, where he had more followers, and where he would be closer to the Umayyad leaders who were driven out of Basra on the tip of the Persian Gulf. In Damascus, meanwhile, Mu'āwiyā, a prominent member of the Umayyad clan, had taken charge. He had managed to rise to prominence while working for Othman, despite the fact that his father had once been Muhammad's greatest enemy. Mu'āwiyā did what he could to make up for the past: he had made great conquests for Islam, and his powerful government in Syria worked to everyone's benefit. Now,

A close-up of one of the walls of the Dome of the Rock in Jerusalem. The building is decorated with colored tiles.

1103

however, what was needed was to avenge Othman's murder. Mu'āwiyā and his fighters took off in the direction of the Euphrates. In Mesopotamia, or Iraq, as the Arabs already called it, Ali had built up a position of power. The garrisons of Basra and Al-Kufa were at his side and, throughout the Islamic community, believers backed him. Mu'āwiyā ruled Syria and could count on the governor of Egypt. Even some of Ali's former opponents had joined him, as well.

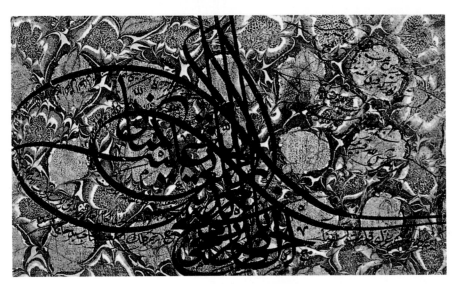

An autograph
of an Ottoman sultan

The two parties clashed at Siffin during a three-day battle. On the third day, Mu'āwiyā appeared to have lost. His soldiers, with copies of the Koran on the points of their lances, screamed their belief that the Book, not the sword, would decide the outcome of the battle. The devout Muslim Ali responded immediately. He and Mu'āwiyā each named a representative to decide, within six months, who had the right to be caliph. Meanwhile, the leaders returned to their bases. The representatives eventually ruled against both parties. Ali refused to accept the decision and continued to fight.

Pious Muslims looked on the dispute as harmful to their religion, therefore totally unacceptable. At almost the same hour, on the same Friday, Mu'āwiyā and Ali were stabbed with poison daggers in their separate mosques. Mu'āwiyā recovered, but Ali died after a few days.

The Muslims from Al-Kufa immediately appointed Ali's son Hassan caliph. But, unlike his father, Hassan had no interest in leadership. He was happy to yield the position to Mu'āwiyā in exchange for all the money he wanted. He returned to Medina, where he was poisoned by a female servant.

Mu'āwiyā was left the undisputed leader

Arab horsemen
from northern Egypt.
Miniature from the *Makamat*
by al-Hariri

1104

Interior of the great mosque in Damascus. Originally a part of this building was a small Christian basilica dedicated to John the Baptist.

of Islam. He ruled as caliph for the rest of his life from Damascus. Ali's second son, Hussein, died tragically as well. Twenty years after the death of their father, Hussein decided to go to Al-Kufa to take over the caliphate. The garrison received the pretender with suspicion. Mu'āwiyā's son sent out an army to stop him. Encountering Hussein and seventy members of his family and staff at Karbala, it slaughtered them all. The date was October 10, 680, a date still remembered in Muslim countries today, when large numbers of people go to Karbala each year to witness a reenactment of the massacre.

## The Shiites

The murder of Hussein immortalized his cause. The rights of Ali, Muhammad's son-in-law, were not forgotten. Huge numbers of Muslims regard Mu'āwiyā and his family as murderous usurpers, violators of the Koran, since the spirit of Muhammad was inherited, they say, by Ali. His chivalry, Hassan's amiability, and Hussein's sacrifice are remembered with the greatest of respect by millions of believers. Ali's followers formed the Shiite sect, whose major tenet is Ali's right

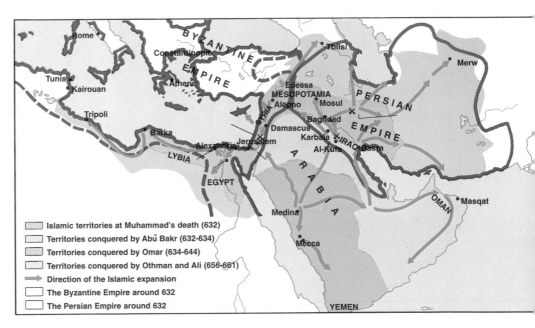

Islamic territories at Muhammad's death (632)
Territories conquered by Abū Bakr (632-634)
Territories conquered by Omar (634-644)
Territories conquered by Othman and Ali (656-661)
Direction of the Islamic expansion
The Byzantine Empire around 632
The Persian Empire around 632

to the leadership of Islam. This created a great schism within Islam. The Shiites developed their own theology and legal system, emphasizing Ali's right to the caliphate as one chosen rather than elected. What entitles him to that position, they say, is his role as the first to convert to Islam and, as important, his marriage to Fatima, Muhammad's

The spread of Islam during the first caliphates (632–661)

1105

The courtyard of the great mosque in Aleppo (Syria). The original building dates from the eighth century.

daughter. The Shiites do not speak of a caliph, but of an *imam* (which means leader of the community). It is used in reference to Islamic holy men. Shiites believe that a series of twelve imans, descended from Ali and Fatima, had the right to the leadership of the Muslims. According to the Shiites, the last iman disappeared, to return at the end of the world.

## Conversions

Despite all the disputes, the power of the Arabs continued to grow. The last resistance of the Persians was finally broken. The Byzantine army was forced back to the mountains of Asia Minor, their attempts to recover their lost land coming to nothing. The Syrians and the Egyptians were under Islamic rule. The question was whether the new subjects would now also assume a belief in Allah. The religion of Muhammad offered more than just theological advantages. There was more than spiritual opportunity in taking up the Koran. Conversion relieved people of the necessity of paying head tax, and Islamic law stipulated that believers could not be slaves. Slowly but surely the great majority of the conquered people made their choice, even adopting the language of their conquerors. Coptic and Aramaic gave way to Arabic. This conversion did not happen

Illustration from a fifteenth-century manuscript. The three men portrayed have been very important to Spain. The one on the left is Tarik.

overnight. There was no such thing as a sudden changeover to Islam. There are tales of entire villages that moved to Christian Asia Minor, protected by Byzantine swords. Many people continued to hold on to their old beliefs. In Syria, Christian churches still exist, and Egypt and Ethiopia have groups of faithful Coptic Christians.

## To the West

The Arabs were not content with Syria and Egypt. Their warriors continued westward. One by one they took over the support points established by Justinian over a century before where the population had long wished to cast off the corrupt government of Constantinople. The Arabs were met with active support by the Berbers from the Atlas Mountains. Toward the end of the seventh century, they had reached the Atlantic Ocean, which seemed to be a natural boundary. But slightly farther north, divided from Africa only by a narrow strait, lay the inter-

nally divided kingdom of the Visigoths. They seemed like easy prey.

In 711, the formidable general Tarik crossed the strait, seizing the fortress that has borne his name ever since: Gibraltar, the rock of Tarik. From there the Bedouin marched on Spain. King Roderick assembled a great army, but it, including the king himself, was cut down immediately by the Muslims.

Within a few years, the reign of the Visigoths was over. Only in the inhospitable north of Spain were they able to hold on. They laid the basis there for a few small kingdoms from where, centuries later, they would organize their reconquest.

The Muslims, not content with Spain alone, now looked toward the fertile countries that stretched northward on the other side of the Pyrenees Mountains. There was no reason to assume that the Franks, who ruled there, could resist them any better than the vanquished Visigoths. Arab gangs began

The mosque of
Al-Kufa (Iraq), which
was built in
the seventh century

The Byzantines were very successful in using the notorious "Greek fire" against the Arabs. This Byzantine miniature shows a battle in which this mysterious weapon is being used.

plundering in Aquitania, and the Christian population soon came to expect Islamic raids on their territory. In 732, however, a great army of horsemen appeared on the plains of Aquitania. It was clear that this time the Arabs were out for more than treasures.

Power in the Frankish Empire was in the hands of the very competent *maior domus* (mayor of the palace) Charles Martel (the Hammer). In contrast to the Visigothic Empire, the Frankish one was fairly homogeneous. Gentlemen and their servants spoke the same language and had the same beliefs. Most of the population believed that protecting the empire was worth the trouble. Charles Martel encountered his adversaries at Poitiers, deep in Aquitania. After seven days of reconnaissance, the Arabs attacked. The determined Franks awaited them. They literally beat off the Arabs, standing fast and making no attempt to gain ground or pursue fleeing Arabs. As the evening came, their ranks were still unbroken. It was as though the Arabs had encountered a stone wall. When it was too dark to fight, the Arabs ceased their attacks. The next day, it became obvious that they had taken advantage of the darkness and disappeared. They withdrew to the other side of the Pyrenees. Perhaps the unintimidated Franks saved the rest of Europe on the plains of Poitiers. In the Pyrenees, a centuries-long border war began. Christians and Muslims carried out raids on each other. There were bloody confrontations. Areas like the French Roussillon became nearly uninhabitable through the constant conflict, but the Arabs could not take over the Frankish Empire.

In the north of Spain, the Christians con-

tinued their bitter battle. After the tenth century, their successful defense began to change over to a slow retrieval of their lost territories. The *Reconquista* (reclamation) had begun. It would determine Spanish and Portuguese history for the rest of the Middle Ages.

## To the East

In the east, too, the battle raged. The Arab armies, having consolidated their power in the Persian Empire, marched forward along the routes once taken by Alexander's troops. They reached the Indus River in 712, at the same time that Tarik crossed the straits to Spain.

In the north, they overthrew parts of Turkestan. They took over the legendary city of Samarkand and beat their way to the Chinese border posts. There the Arab soldiers had to test their strength against an army of Central Asia. The battle ended in a tie, and here, too, the Arabs made no more attempts to press their power further.

## Fortress Constantinople

Meanwhile, the Eastern Roman Empire continued to stand like a massive stone wall between Europe and the onslaughts of the Muslim warriors. The empire had been reduced to the Balkan Peninsula and Asia Minor, but there its royal soldiers held on with the strength of the desperate. Another threat appeared, a navy mounted by the Arabs. It broke the naval monopoly of the Byzantines in the Mediterranean within a few years. The Arabs proved to be excellent sailors, sending fleets to terrorize the Christians in every coastal realm. The

Byzantine emperor was forced off the island of Cyprus and found control of the Aegean Sea increasingly difficult.

In 674, the Arabs attempted to invade Constantinople. The fleet approached the great domed city, but the people of Constantinople stood courageously behind their church and their emperor, keeping the Arabs out of Constantinople. The battles went on for five years without significant victory on either side. As if on schedule, the Arabs showed up to fight in Constantinople every spring.

The Byzantines made use of a new

Miniature from the fourteenth century depicting the main character from the *Makamat* by al-Hariri delivering a sermon in the mosque of Samarkand

1109

weapon known as Greek fire. Its origin and composition remain unknown to this day. The Byzantines kept its formula secret, but from descriptions of it, we know approximately how it worked. The soldiers sprayed a sticky fluid on the enemy ships that ignited spontaneously and could not be extin-

Remains
of a mosque in
Samarkand

guished with water. Only urine and sand, it appeared, could put it out. Innumerable Arab ships and crews went up in flames. Modern scholars have concluded that the fluid contained phosphorus, but do not know exactly how the Byzantines managed to control this sort of weaponry, since phosphorus ignites as soon as it comes into contact with oxygen. The Byzantines could have used airtight storage containers, if that had not been technically impossible at the time. Greek fire remains a mystery.

### Leo III, the Isaurian (ca. 680–741)

Toward the end of the seventh century, the Arabs withdrew, only to begin a new wave of expansion at the beginning of the eighth century. In 717, Arab hordes again stormed into the Byzantine Empire. Once again, the Islamic generals prepared to attack the capital. This time, they boxed in Constantinople, setting a huge army in place in front of its walls and closing off its harbors with a gigantic fleet.

However, control of the city was in the hands of the general, Leo. Reigning as Leo III and called the Isaurian, he had just deposed the Byzantine emperor Theodosius III. He had put an end to the series of turbulent successions that had troubled the Byzantine Empire for years. A skilled domestic political leader, he was also an excellent diplomat. He had managed to win the Bulgarians, notable warriors, to his side. They now attacked the Arab army with great success. Leo was also a fine military tactician. He had ordered a heavy chain stretched underwater in the bay called the Golden Horn. Scores of Arabian ships were caught on it, ready to be torched by the Greek fire. The siege of Constantinople had to be lifted. Although the Arabs continued to invade Anatolia, they did not again attack the capital city. It would remain free for centuries.

Leo III was a notable emperor. The Isaurian dynasty he founded held power until 802. He established a legal code in Greek, called the Ecloga, that would last two hundred years. Ten years before his death, he was excommunicated by the pope for his ban on the use of icons in Christian worship. This created a theological controversy over *iconoclasm* (from the Greek *eikon*, image, and *klaein*, break) that would last for centuries.

Leo III reorganized the army into an elite force called the *tagmata* and a regular corps called *themata*. A commanding officer called a *stratēgos* was appointed for each and given civil, as well as military authority. The empire was divided into army districts and the soldiers given tax-exempt land. Leo was thus able to maintain a powerful military without the cost of the salaried army that had strained imperial resources in the past. He completed his reign with successful campaigns into Asia Minor. He could do little about the war-induced decline of agriculture in the rural areas and of education and commerce everywhere outside Thessaloniki and Constantinople, but by the time of his death, he had made his empire safe. Although he had not been able to regain Syria and Egypt, he had made the shrunken Byzantine state a sturdy bulwark against Islamic expansion. Only when new people took the reins of power in the Islamic world would Constantinople again find itself in danger.

Silk tapestry, made at the court of the Abbasids in the second half of the tenth century

# The Caliphs

## *The First Rulers of the Arab World*

Othman (or Uthman ibn Affan), an original convert of Muhammad and third caliph, was assassinated in 656. He had aroused the enmity of many Muslims for his favoritism of the aristocrats of Mecca and his order to destroy all versions of the Koran other than the one he issued. Muslims from Medina and the army proclaimed Ali, a cousin and son-in-law of Muhammad, as the fourth caliph. Those recognizing his authority and that of his descendants to rule are called the Shiites. Mu'āwiyā the governor of Syria, refusing to recognize Ali, first fought him and then, jointly with him, submitted the case for arbitration in 657. Some of Ali's followers, a group called the Kharijites, were enraged at his acquiescence to arbitration. Their attempt to kill both parties resulted only in the death of Ali.

In 661, the Muslims from the city of Al-Kufa appointed Hassan as caliph. He was the grandson of Muhammad, the son of Ali and Muhammad's daughter Fatima. Mu'āwiyā paid Hassan to retire to Medina, taking over himself as leader of the believers. That transaction, in some sense, also retired the Bedouin from political power. Medina itself became a holy city outside the center of power, its sites visited by pilgrims, scholars, and wealthy potential successors to Hassan.

Mu'āwiyā was a member of the aristocratic clan of caravan merchants called the Umayya. He established the first great caliphate dynasty, the Umayyads, moving his capital to Damascus, centrally located within the newly formed empire. The move gave the Muslims significantly greater expo-

1111

Gold coin from the Umayyad caliph Abd al-Malik, who reigned from 685 to 705

sure to the advanced culture and government of the Byzantine Empire.

Although his dynasty would rule for less than a century, Mu'āwiyā laid the groundwork for a political system that would dominate the Islamic world for some five hundred years. His own approach to power resembled that of a potentate in the capitals of Byzantine Constantinople or Persian Ctesiphon than that of the Muslims Omar or Muhammad. He ruled with the aid of favorites who obtained their positions more on the basis of family connection or flattery than ability. Corruption and intrigue were endemic in his court, yet Mu'āwiyā was a talented sovereign, able to assess problems quickly and take action as necessary. His orders were carried out by civilian and military personnel alike, but he planted the seeds of decay that would threaten the Islamic world.

## The Umayyad Dynasty (661–750)

After Mu'āwiyā died, there were no succession problems. Before his death, he had named his son Yazid as his successor, setting a precedent followed by the rest of his dynasty. While this increased the stability of the empire, it was objected to by the majority of Muslims, called Sunnites. These were the followers of the *Sunnah* (Islamic custom) called the Way of the Prophet. They contended that the principles laid down by the first four "rightly guided" caliphs, all original converts of Muhammad, should be followed. They insisted that the caliph be a member of the Quraysh tribe of Muhammad and that he be elected to office by a council of Muslim elders. The Umayyads made succession the prerogative of their own family, although they did at least require the council of elders to support the heir they chose.

The Sunnites also insisted that the caliph

enforce Koranic law and foster the spread of Islam. Here, the Umayyads failed. In the less than hundred years they ran the empire, they gained a reputation for great degeneracy. Scandalous stories circulated. It was said that one prince was accustomed to swimming in wine. At the court in Damascus, a sophisticated, cosmopolitan atmosphere reigned, at odds with Muslim orthodoxy. Islam forbid the drinking of alcoholic beverages, yet even under Yazid, wine was in common use in the palace. The Umayyads granted high positions to Christians and offered court sponsorship to artists, even if they were nonbelievers. The great Arab poet Al-Akhtal, a skeptical Arab Monophysite, was one of the caliph's personal friends, although his views certainly did not fit with those of the Koran. Monophysitism, from the Greek *monos* (single) and *physis* (nature), contended that Jesus Christ had only a single nature, which was divine, not human. This conflicted with both the Christian doctrine that Christ was both divine and human and the Muslim doctrine that he was only as human as all the other prophets, including Muhammad.

The tolerance shown at court may have been seen as moral laxity by righteous Muslims, but it created room for the growth of an Arabian culture. Poetry, art, and architecture flourished at the court of the Umayyads. Its architects transformed St. John's Basilica into a mosque, which is still one of the most beautiful in the east. Artists, probably including many Byzantines, added new designs to the palaces and the residences of the wealthy. These decorations were permitted under the Koran (which forbids the representation of figures). The city of Damascus itself realized an unprecedented boom. Under the Byzantines, it had never

been more than an important fortress. After the fall of Antioch in one of the many wars against the Persians, the city had begun to expand as an urban center. Now, as the Umayyad capital, it became the center of an immense world empire. Merely the fact that more caravans than ever before traveled to it gave trade and craftsmanship an economic boost. Its thousand-year-old Main Street became comparable to the Mesè in Constantinople, a place where the *dirhams* (currency) flowed among the merchants. The weavers of Damascus developed a new technique that made it possible to produce a firm, lustrous patterned fabric named "Damask," a name still used for the same weave. Damascus seemed destined to become the glittering center of a stable empire, but the dynasty of the Umayyads would succumb to revolution. Imperial power would shift east to a new metropolis, Baghdad, in Iraq.

Yazid I succeeded his father as caliph in 680, reigning only until 683. He was opposed by both the Meccans and the Shiites of Al-Kufa. The Al-Kufa contingent recognized only Hussein, Ali's second son and grandson of Muhammad, as caliph. Hussein was killed on the plain of Karbala, in Iraq. The Meccan rebellion continued until stopped by Abd al-Malik, caliph from 685 to 705.

### Revolution

Over the eighth century, the Umayyads problems increased. Their tax policies created dissatisfaction even among their own followers. Their *jihad* (holy war) failed against the Byzantines. The Carolingian Charles Martel and his Frankish army defeated them in 732.

Meanwhile, a new group of recent, but dissatisfied non-Arabic converts formed, called the *mawali* in Arabic. They claimed that their acceptance of the Koran had failed to gain them civil rights in the Islamic state. Arabs close to the caliph regarded them as inferior, second-rate Muslims. Opposition grew, with points of support not only in the Hejaz but in Persia. There, great masses of people had abandoned their traditional Zoroastrianism for Islam and discrimination was strongly felt. (Founded by Zoroaster, and detailed in the scriptures called the *Zend-Avesta*, this older religion posited competing spirits of good and evil. Like Islam, it offered belief in an afterlife.)

No matter how powerful the leadership of the Umayyads was, and how quickly its economy developed, the division caused by the Umayyad accession to power and the defeat of the followers of Ali resurfaced. The Shiites had not forgotten the downfall of Ali and his sons. They aimed for a restoration of the old caliphate. Time and again the Umayyads were forced to subdue uprisings. The garrison cities of Al-Kufa and Bara lived in constant discord. The Hejaz, the coastal area where Mecca is located, grew increasingly restless as the Shiites gained followers.

Dynastic battles that had long played a role within Arab armies began to escalate dangerously. Each new succession in the palace of Damascus was the impetus for a whole series of murders, involving even inaccessible garrison towns. The last Umayyads lacked the skill to keep the battling forces in balance. The empire began to disintegrate.

A contender for succession to the caliphate, appeared about 718: the distinguished family called the Abbasids, descended from Muhammad's uncle Abbas. As time went on, increasing numbers of Muslims favored a change of power and the Abbasid dynasty.

In Persia, meanwhile, an extremely clever politician was keeping himself busy with all kinds of subversive activities. This was the convert Abu Muslim, who had personally experienced discrimination by the Arabs. As a fervent Shiite, he was glad to use the Abbasids as a tool to stir up the population. By 747, he and the converts, as well as Iranian and non-Muslim groups dissatisfied with the Umayyads, recognized Abū al-'Abbās as caliph. They had the support in northern Persia to succeed, although it took three years to do so. Under Abu Muslim, who proved himself to be a brilliant general, the combined forces defeated the Umayyad army.

### The Abbasids of Baghdad (750–1258)
*Abū al-'Abbās as-Saffāh, Caliph (750–754)*
Abū al-'Abbās as-Saffāh had most of the Umayyad family executed. Only a single member escaped. The action gave him his nickname: As-Saffah, the Bloodshedder. He proved to be very different than what Abu

Iranian bowl
in the shape of a human
figure, from the
tenth century

Persian miniature
depicting a Muslim ruler
administering justice
in the garden of his palace.
A couple of servants in
the foreground carry
out his verdicts.

1114

Abū al-'Abbās receives his followers' oaths of fidelity in the mosque at Al-Kufa. Persian miniature from the fifteenth century

Muslim had thought. The new caliph evidently did not plan to put the Shiite ideals into practice. On the contrary, he frequently betrayed both the ideals and individual Shiites, taking whatever action he considered politically expedient. Abū al-Abbās did not rule for long. After his death it appeared, for a while, that his dynasty would not last.

### Al-Mansur, Caliph (754–755)

A bitter civil war broke out in which Abu Muslim fought side by side with Abū al-'Abbās's brother, Al-Mansur. It was largely due to Abu Muslim's military ability that Al-Mansur was able to take over as the new caliph. Once in office and possibly fearing Abu Muslim's potential as a rival, he had the great general killed.

Al-Mansur moved the imperial capital to Iraq, where the Umayyads had incurred many enemies. On the Tigris River, he built a metropolis which he gave the poetic name "City of Peace". The designation was never generally accepted. The people called it by

A man is given a massage by a servant. Miniature painting from the fifteenth century

the name of a neighboring village, Baghdad.

The relocation of the capital city was more than symbolic. Baghdad is quite a bit farther from the Arabian desert than Damascus and a lot closer to Persia. Abū al-ʿAbbās did not make the mistake of alienating the new converts there. It is sometimes said that the Abbasid conquest was actually a Persian one. While it is true that there were many Persian court ceremonies at the caliph's court in Baghdad and also true that the Persians won a significant amount of power, there was no question of a power takeover. Baghdad was an Arabian city. Its people, like its court, spoke Arabic, not Persian.

Al-Mansur proved to be an energetic administrator, consolidating the people and the power of the caliphate. He reorganized

The tower of al-Maluiyyah was formerly the minaret of the mosque of Samarra (Iraq), that was founded by Al-Mustasim. Access is gained by walking up a ramp that wraps around the tower.

Camel feeding her foal,
as painted on a ninth-century
Samarran bowl

the bureaucracy, initiating a policy of cultural tolerance that would be consistently carried out by his successors. He attempted to unite his subjects on the basis of their shared religion rather than forcing an Arabic civilization on them. He wanted his people observing Islam, but attempted to avoid favoritism. Contending that all believers were equal before God, he treated no one inequitably, especially the Arabs.

The caliph lived in the greatest of style. The last traces of tribal sheik simplicity disappeared. Al-Mansur began the building of a palace complex which, at its largest point, would have a circumference of almost two miles (3.2 kilometers). Transcending Damascus as a center of trade, craftsmanship, and culture, the new capital city soon rivaled only Byzantium.

The Persian ceremonies that were introduced at the court separated the caliph from his subjects. He lived in isolation in fairytale luxury, learning only via his intermediaries what was happening outside the palace gates. Born in a closed harem surrounded by women of many nationalities and used to the intrigues of court atmosphere, as ruler he was comfortable being surrounded by sycophants and schemers.

Al-Mansur was well aware that he could not afford to lose his popularity with the people. For this reason he had his court employ poets to propagandize in song about his deeds as a great caliph. Anecdotes were circulated that accented the favorable aspects of his character, portraying him as a pious and simple Muslim who made sure that justice was served and that the weaker members of society were protected. This campaign was continued by Al-Mansur's successors. None was as successful in this regard as Harun Al-Rashid.

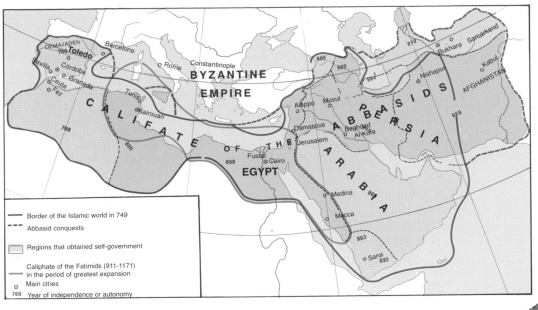

The Islamic world from 750 to 1055

Border of the Islamic world in 749

Abbasid conquests

Regions that obtained self-government

Caliphate of the Fatimids (911-1171) in the period of greatest expansion

○ Main cities

760 Year of independence or autonomy

### Harun Al-Rashid, Caliph (786–809)

Under Harun Al-Rashid and his son, Abdullah al-Mamun, the caliphate of the Abbasids reached its peak. Building on the work of their predecessors, they encouraged education and the arts, inviting foreign intellectuals to the court for lectures and debate. Harun Al-Rashid, notable for his short temper, was an able diplomat nonetheless, exchanging ambassadors with Charlemagne, the first Holy Roman emperor.

### Abdullah al-Mamun, Caliph (813–830)

Shortly after Harun Al-Rashid's reign, theological problems arose with the Sunnite Muslims. They claimed that the Koran was infallible, the eternal word of God, revealed to Muhammad rather than being created by him. Al-Mamun, who had succeeded his father in 813 as the new caliph, resisted this idea. He instituted a purification of the entire civil service, a sort of inquisition, making all officials swear under oath that the Koran had been created.

Al-Mamun's government, despite its persecution of the Sunnites, established a Golden Age of science and literature. According to Muslim chronicles of the era, Aristotle himself appeared before the caliph in a dream, advising him to study Greek science. The caliph enthusiastically complied, and began to collect ancient manuscripts. He sent off emissaries to Constantinople to get the writings of Plato, Aristotle, Archimedes,

King from a set of chess pieces that supposedly belonged to caliph Harun Al-Rashid

1119

The mosque
of Ibn Tulum in Cairo.
It was built in 879,
after the mosque
of Samarra

and the other scholars he had heard about, and then had them translated into Arabic. In Baghdad, he had a house of *hikma* (science) built, which provided researchers with an outstanding library. As he gradually yielded educational, political, and administrative control to the functionaries whose positions he had established, he adopted a stronger role in protecting his concept of Islam from heretical attack.

### Abbasid Decline

After Al-Mamun, the political power of the caliphs began to decline. They delegated increasing administrative authority to government officials and began to lose control of their own guards. At the same time, the religious activity of the caliphs increased. Regarding themselves as defenders of Islam, they encouraged the popular persecution of nonbelievers. The Abbasids were widely resented outside Baghdad.

In the eastern provinces, a number of rebel leaders declared independence, establishing their own principalities. The Shiites estab-

lished their own caliphate in North Africa. Over the ninth and tenth centuries, other independent caliphates were formed in northern Africa and Spain. The empire shrank inside the borders of Iraq, governing, in essence, only Baghdad, as rebelling black slaves took over the southern part of the country. The Abbasid caliphate degenerated as the role of caliphs was gradually reduced to purely religious matters. By the middle of the tenth century, the Abbasids remained only at the pleasure of the military, the caliph carrying out only ceremonial tasks.

Baghdad was ruled by a state official called the "Prince of Princes." In 945, control of that government position fell into the hands of a Shiite dynasty, giving the persecuted sect its long-sought goal. Al-Mustasim, a fellow believer, was made the new prince of princes, giving the Shiites the potential to realize their ideals. However, he belonged to a moderate wing of the faction and did not wish to practice any radical politics. The Shiites, suspecting betrayal, refused to recognize his government.

## Turks

A new group of Turks, called the Seljuks, flooded the country about the same time. The conversion of the Turks to Islam had brought them into the Arabian culture, but they had retained their own language and customs. Under their leaders, called sultans, the Turks had acquired great influence on the country's administration. Turkic power grew as the potentates of the small kingdoms throughout the empire fought each other.

Now the Turks took over Baghdad, reinvigorating the caliphate and forcing the Shiites into opposition again. The Shiites, all claiming to be followers of Ali, divided into groups of various size. No longer able to organize large-scale strategy, they adopted what they saw as the only tactic left to them: terrorism. The Shiite guerrillas kept the Seljuks constantly on guard against their murderous attacks.

Ultimately, the downfall of the Abbasid dynasty came not from the Shiites but from forces quite foreign to the Middle Eastern world. In 1258, the Mongol Hulegu Khan, grandson of Genghis Khan, sacked Baghdad, ending five centuries of Abbasid rule. Two members of the Abbasid dynasty managed to escape to Egypt. They were taken in by the Mamluk sultan Baybars I. He named them both, in succession, as caliph but allowed them only religious authority, not political.

### The Fatimids of Cairo (909–1517)

On the northern coast of Africa, in the city of Tunis, very far from the center of the empire and virtually independent for centuries, militant Shiites seized the chance to establish a countercaliphate. The patriarch of the new dynasty was Ubayd Allah, who proclaimed himself caliph in Tunisia in 909. He claimed to have descended from Fatima, the only daughter of Muhammad who survived him. His caliphate, named for her, was called the Fatimid.

The Fatimids acquired a large following in North Africa. Once they had taken control of Egypt, they established a new capital city at Cairo, on the Nile, close to the old town of Fustat. The official year of its establishment was 969, a favorable time for a competing capital. The Fatimids had just then reached the apex of their power. Iraq was being torn apart by Turkish fratricidal struggles. The power of the caliph in Baghdad had become negligible as his city was decaying rapidly. Damascus was unable to regain its old position.

Cairo, in some sense, was forced to become a metropolis, to the delight of the Fatimids. They were eager to make their empire the center of all Islam. They were

delighted when they got the China and India trade that normally went to Baghdad. An earthquake destroyed the harbor city of Siraf in the Persian Gulf, forcing the traders to divert their shipping routes to the Red Sea, much closer to Cairo. Fatimid commerce benefited greatly.

The caliphate of the Fatimids was less glorious than that of the Abbasids or the Umayyads. Its caliph in Cairo was unable to maintain law and order without the use of mercenaries. Yet by the end of the tenth century, at the height of its power, the Fatimids

Bronze griffin made during the reign of the Fatimids (tenth century)

1121

controlled northern Africa from Egypt west to what is now Algeria, up the eastern Mediterranean coast to Syria, and the island of Sicily. Because of their claim to be directly descended from Ali and Fatima, the son-in-law and daughter of Muhammad, they considered themselves to be in possession of

A doctor feels the pulse of a sick man in a Persian garden while his assistants in the foreground are already busy preparing medicines.

divine truth, sinless and infallible. Their missionaries roamed the Muslim world, converting followers of Shism. This made them both a theological and political threat to the Sunnite Abbasid caliphate in Baghdad. In 1171, Saladin, the sultan of Egypt, overthrew the Fatimids.

### The Umayyads of Córdoba (929–1031)
Abd al-Rahmōn was the only Umayyad who escaped the family massacre at the hands of

Abū al-'Abbās, the Abbasid Bloodshedder, in 755. He fled to the west, ending up in Spain. He removed the provincial governor of Córdoba by force of arms and took over his position. Abd al-Rahmōn made a great concession to the Abbasids: he recognized their right to the caliphate.

The Abbasid caliphs never made any attempt to prove their might in the far west. Spain was, in some sense, the territorial price that Abū al-'Abbās paid for the caliphate. The Umayyads in Spain, resenting the new dynasty despite their recognition of it, continued to believe their family had an unalienable right to the caliphate. However, to avoid bringing trouble upon themselves, they did not challenge the power of Baghdad for almost two centuries. Only when the realm of the Abbasids collapsed into anarchy did the Umayyads dare put their presumptions into practice. In 929, Abd al-Rahmōn III named himself caliph, apparently inspired by the Fatimid example.

The caliphate of Córdoba collapsed less than a century later. Spain disintegrated into a number of small, mutually competitive Islamic states. The situation made it easy for the Christians to reconquer the entire Iberian Peninsula. Around 1200, the *Reconquista* (reconquest) was complete, though it would take until 1492 before the last Muslim sovereign, the ruler of Granada, was forced to withdraw to North Africa.

### The Caliphate
The caliphs, proud rulers of a once immense empire, eventually lost even their freedom. Almost the whole Arab world fell to Turkish conquest. Wherever Muslim rule prevailed, competing kings adopted the title of caliph for centuries with no particular regard for its original requirements. The title was common in the Ottoman Empire but only stressed for its religious importance when the ruling sultans wanted the backing of Muslims against their Christian enemies. After World War I brought down the Ottoman Empire in 1918, Turkish nationalists overthrew both the sultan and the caliph. The Grand National Assembly of Turkey formally abolished the caliphate in March 1924.

The title of caliph (and direct descent from Muhammad) was claimed by Husayn ibn Al, king of the Hejaz, the region conquered in 1925 by Abdul Aziz ibn Saud, now part of Saudi Arabia. There has been no international Muslim consensus on reestablishing a caliphate.

Earthenware bowl depicting an aristocrat during a hunting party, made in Iran (twelfth century)

# The Riches of Islam

*The Flourishing of Trade, Science, and Craftsmanship*

In the period of the caliphs (656–1031), western Europe was an underdeveloped area. North of the Pyrenees stretched a realm where impoverished farmers pried scanty harvests from the soil, ghostlike ruins of cities reminded them of lost prosperity, and Christians could only remember past greatness. The civilized rulers of Muslim Córdoba might have seen themselves as bringing civilization to the pathetic barbarians.

Charles Martel's conquest of the Muslims at Poitiers in 732 may have saved European Christian culture from the infidel, but it perpetuated the economic status quo for centuries. Not until four hundred years later could one speak of progress, and that was due largely to Arab influences.

1123

Detail of an ivory box,
made in the eleventh century,
probably in Egypt
or Spain

## Dirhams

Mu'āwiyā was the representative of a mercantile dynasty that gave its name to the caliphate he founded: the Umayyad. He changed the emphasis of the caliphs managing Muhammad's legacy from religious idealism to mercantilism and trade. The Arabs had conquered a prosperous part of the world. Their expansion was, to a great extent, at the expense of the Persian and Byzantine Empires. Particularly in Constantinople, the ancient money economy had been well maintained. It had not disintegrated into innumerable self-contained and competitive areas. Half of this rich and well-developed state fell, within a few years, into Arab hands. The conquerors were able to take over their new holdings with few problems, quickly integrating the region into the rest of their empire. The Arabs were able to get their empire off to a better start than the Franks had in their deteriorated and war-plagued Gaul.

The caliphs were powerful rulers. They saw to it that their enormous empire was effectively governed. It extended from their settlement at the mouth of the Tagus River at Lisbon to the unassailable border fortresses

The inside of a
decorated Iranian bowl
from the thirteenth
century

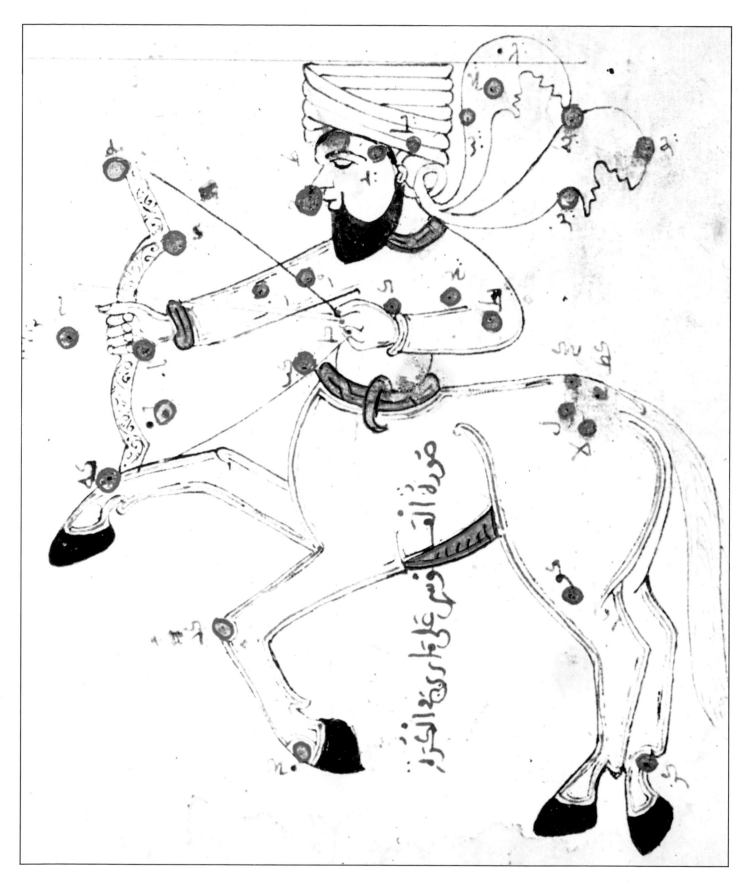

منطقة البروج
قوس الرامي الذي يستعمل القوس

of China. They could develop not only safe roads, but an economy that covered entire hemispheres, providing the Muslim producer the assurance of a reasonable distribution area for his products. Even the civil wars that plagued the Islamic world never actually disrupted its economic traffic. It faced no loss of economic integrity until the year 1000. Only then was economic unity lost, with the Muslims seeing the kind of structural decay Christianity was just managing to overcome.

## Agriculture

The Arab economy was based on and

The constellation of Sagittarius, an illustration on a page from a manuscript about the stars by As-Sufi

A group of Arabs rides into an Arabian town on their camels. An Arab miniature painting from *Makamat* by al-Hariri

autonomous economies developed. In the Islamic world, the opposite was the case. There, more and more dirhams appeared on the market, which made economic ties among the various regions ever stronger.

The Islamic farmer and manufacturer did not produce food and necessities for himself or a landlord. He grew and sold products for an active market, sometimes thousands of miles from his land. Textiles provide a good example. They were woven in patterns and styles unique to various cities or regions. The mousseline fabric of Mosul was sought after around the world. The same applied to the damask cloth of Damascus and the fustian from Egypt's Fustat.

Islamic conquerors introduced the growing of sugar cane and cotton to other countries, hastening the progress of agriculture. Sugar and textiles are also durable goods that can be readily transported and can tolerate long journeys. In a time of slow transportation, this is especially important. Agriculture, then, became intricately intertwined in the mercantile economy.

## Caravans

"Islam is the desert," writes the Islamic essayist Essad Bey. The sand dunes of Arabia or the immense Sahara were the domain of the Muslim believer, who were not limited by the lack of water and the burning sun. Indeed, the Muslim knew the desert and how to survive there. While the residents of cultural areas near the sea, or along broad rivers, saw the desert as dangerous, an impenetrable barrier, for the Bedouin it was a connecting road. The Arabs who spilled all over the world knew how to travel on that road. The deserts of the east became the arteries of the immense Arabian Empire.

The Bedouin were the first to tame the camel. They knew the animal as a tough creature that could survive in dry areas, thanks to the fatty humps on its back. It is outstandingly suited to serving man on his treks through the desert. The camel does not actually live on less water than other animals, it simply needs to drink much less regularly. The female camel produces milk with a particularly high fat content. The camel's meat is edible and its hide can be made into warm blankets essential to the Bedouin in the cold desert nights. As a beast of burden, the camel is without equal. It is capable of carrying up to 220 pounds (100 kilograms) on its back through the desert, for weeks at a time. The Bedouin owed their lives and their livelihood to their camels.

Traders had discovered the value of camels very early, using them in long caravans for safety and greater profit. The politi-

remained linked to agriculture. The merchants and the craftsmen in the Arab world were completely dependent upon agricultural products, since no one could produce as much and as fast as a farmer.

Arabian agriculture differed fundamentally from that of the isolated west where people grew things primarily for their own use. In the west, the circulation of money often came to a standstill, as ever smaller

cal unity that the Arabs brought to a huge area advanced caravan traffic to a high degree. There was no longer a restless Persian-Byzantine border area. Even more important, the Persian and Byzantine tax collectors had disappeared. The taxes of the theocratic caliphs were a relief compared to the oppressive systems of the earlier rulers.

A well-organized caravan had the characteristics of a military operation. Its leader and a few aides had unlimited authority. The rules of the trail were precisely formulated and just as precisely followed. One could deviate from the route and the travel plan only in emergencies. The sun, the lack of water, and the blowing sand are too treacher-

Caravan of Arab merchants. Miniature from the *Makamat* by al-Hariri

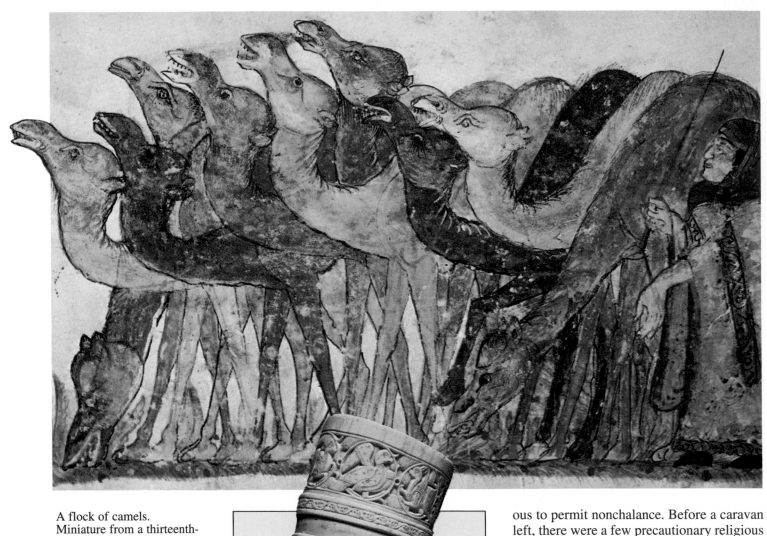

A flock of camels. Miniature from a thirteenth-century Arabian manuscript

An ivory horn from the eleventh century

ous to permit nonchalance. Before a caravan left, there were a few precautionary religious invocations. In addition, its leader would arrange safe passage through the predatory Bedouin by paying a toll that would grant the merchants the "protection" of the desert dwellers. The modern Portuguese word for customs, *alfandega*, is derived from the Arabic word for caravan station. Such stations lay everywhere along caravan routes, usually one day's travel apart. At busy points the stations developed into desert towns with large pavilions and many inns for travelers. Some of these stations, like the one near the modern Aleppo, still exist today.

The destination point of the caravan was one of the large commercial centers of the Arabian world: Baghdad, Damascus, Samarra, or Cairo. There the merchandise was traded, often continuing its journey on the backs of other camels. There was lively trade with India, and the merchants of Turkestan had contact with Chinese traders who brought their silk through the vast Gobi Desert to the borders of Central Asia.

## Sea
The desert was not the only domain of the Islamic merchants. Shortly after Muhammad's death, the first believers dared to trav-

# Arab Philosophy and Learning

Although Persia, India, and Egypt all influenced the development of Arab philosophy and science, it was the Greek philosophers of the classical period who had the greatest impact. In the ninth century the city of Baghdad, which was the capital of the Abbasid caliphs, became a major center for learning. Among the sources that made their way into the intellectual circles in Baghdad were Greek manuscripts, bought from the Byzantines, that were translated into Arabic. These manuscripts included philosophical and scientific treatises.

The theology of Islam further stimulated Arab thinking. Several Arabian thinkers tried to integrate Islamic tradition with Greek philosophy. Their acceptance of the ideas of Aristotle and Plato often brought them into conflict with Islamic theologians, despite the interest of Muslim rulers in the study of liberal arts.

Arab philosophers also played a major role in the reintroduction of Greek philosophy to western Europe. Two of the most famous of them are Avicenna (Ibn Sīnā in Arabic) and Averroës (Ibn Rushd in Arabic).

Avicenna (980–1037) worked as a physician and philosopher. He wrote the *Book of Healing* in which he treated a great number of subjects: logic, the natural sciences, geometry, astronomy, arithmetic, and metaphysics. His thinking in this work owes a great deal to Aristotle and to Neoplatonism. Avicenna also wrote the *Canon of Medicine*, the most famous book in medical history, East and West. It is a systematic encyclopedia based on Greek and Arabian knowledge. It became a standard work, used for centuries in the universities of Europe.

The physician and judge Averroës (1126–1198) also wrote a book on medicine, but the major body of his work dealt with the relation between religious law and philosophy. Because of his unorthodox thinking, both Christians and Muslims considered him a heretic. In the west, Averroës became famous for his lengthy commentaries on Aristotle. These were translated into Latin during the twelfth century and were widely read. They had an enormous influence on the development of philosophy in Europe.

Fifteenth-century miniature from a manuscript called *al-Kanun fi'l-Tibb* by Avicenna. In Arabian, Avicenna was called Abdallah ibn Sīnā, and he lived between 980 and 1037. This work is a summary of classic and Arab medicine.

Map of the world designed by al-Idrisi

The two sides of an astrolabe, made by Ibrahim ben Said Assali

el to the Mediterranean. It was dominated by Byzantine warships. Their original goal was to plunder, and the Bedouin viewed the first expeditions as acts of pure recklessness. But the rich spoils that the first sea travelers brought back made even the greatest skeptics change their minds.

The Arabs became, in short order, a maritime power to be reckoned with. They proved to be brilliant sailors, ousting the Byzantine fleets from the western Mediterranean Sea. In the east, the Byzantines could barely defend their own coasts. Even in the Aegean Sea Muslim fleets pirated the Christian trade ships.

The Muslims ruled the seas. Their fleets could plunder undisturbed. Once their sailors even dared to camp in Ostia, the port of Rome at the mouth of the Tiber. The Italians did not dare fight them, but could only build watchtowers so they could see the ships off the coast in time to issue warnings.

The seagoing Arabs were not limited to piracy. Soon they sent trade ships across the Mediterranean. While they maintained contact with various Muslim harbors, there was hardly any trade with Christians. Relations at the time were far too strained and it may have been more profitable to simply plunder the nonbelievers.

What trade contact did exist between the Muslims and the western European Christians was maintained by traveling Jewish merchants who were not involved in any of the military conflicts prevalent everywhere. The greatest volume of trade was eventually carried on in the basin of the Indian Ocean, because it encompassed wealthy areas and formed a connecting route from one great culture to the other. Huge fleets sailed from the Persian Gulf to the coast of India, where the Arabs had large factories. Loaded with valuable spices, the ships sailed back to their home harbors. These were adventurous voyages that produced a whole collection of tall tales concerning travels to India. The history of Sindbad the sailor from *A Thousand and One Nights* is one such story.

**A Hundred Thousand Camels**

The economy of Islam continued to grow for centuries with trade becoming more and more international and money circulating through more of the population. At a certain point the date trade alone mobilized 100,000 camels. The melon and sugar cane trade were almost as important.

The Arabs were not satisfied with traditional production methods, but looked for improvements. One result was the windmill. This invention saved an enormous amount of human energy. What had once been done in

labor-intensive treadmills could now be left to a simple mechanism. Their ability in technology made the Arabs outstanding craftspeople. The woven textiles from Islamic cities were without equal. Even the studios of Byzantium could not outdo the weavers of Damascus and Mosul. In Spain, smithing developed into a true art. The swords from Córdoba and Toledo were famous throughout the entire Islamic world, feared among the Christians, and traded in Africa. A number of saber makers still live and work in Toledo today, whose ancestors perfected their art through the storms of the reconquistadores.

However, the eastern craftsmen most acclaimed were the carpet makers. Carpet making reached its peak of perfection in Persia and Anatolia. Carpets in beautiful colors and patterns made their way from small villages to the palaces of the mighty. This carpet production, in turn, started a whole dyes industry that was concentrated in the Iraqi Basra. One craft kept the other alive.

The merchants formed a link between the producers and the consumers in the vast empire. They developed an impressive arsenal of sales techniques to protect themselves and their markets. When the Christian merchants were still keeping their administrations in order with great difficulty, their Arabian counterparts were using the much simpler signs that they had taken over from the Indians. Not until the Renaissance would the Europeans adopt the use of the new signs they called Arabian numerals.

The credit industry was developing, too, because merchants did not dare travel carrying great amounts of money. There were far too many robbers waiting for them. They preferred to make use of bills of exchange. This became common in Christian Europe as

Illustration from the *Makamat* by al-Hariri. In the top half of the picture, a merchant weighs a gold coin so that he can make a sale; the bottom half shows a Muslim selecting new servants.

well. In the Arab trade centers, people lent and invested money, they bought shares in caravans, and paid out interest. The money trade in cities such as Córdoba or Baghdad did not differ fundamentally from that of modern centers. Most aspects of today's banking were present in rudimentary form. The Arab economy reached its peak at the end of the eighth century. Two hundred years later, the first symptoms of its demise were already visible. When the Arabs lost control of their empires, the era of their wealth was over and the Islamic world was put on the defensive.

## Change of Social Culture

The takeover by the Abbasids in 750 was a true revolution of the Muslim converts against their Arabian conquerors. It was a huge emancipation movement of Persians, Greeks, Syrians, Egyptians, Berbers, and any other people who were not under the rule of the caliph, bringing back some of the old eastern relationships.

With the Umayyad dynasty, the easygoing nature of the desert dweller disappeared for good. The desert dweller's freedom was virtually unlimited; the Bedouin was anything but servile. Mu'āwiyā often had to confer for hours with his aides to convince them of the validity and purpose of his measures. This turned out to be less true for his successors, though something of that desert democracy continued to prevail. The Muslim army was a relatively independent body, notable for its pride. The soldiers could not be convinced to give up their old tribal loyalties, so that army posts frequently looked more like civil war battlegrounds than bases for disciplined soldiers. Bloody battles took place in every garrison; it is a wonder the Umayyads managed to keep their empire together at all.

After 750, when Abū al-'Abbās took over, this was no longer the case. Nicknamed the Bloodshedder for his massacre of the Umayyad family, he sent the Bedouin back to their old domain, the desert. The caliph then surrounded himself with a coterie of subordinates from Byzantium and the Persian Empire. They had brought with them a different tradition, one of respect for designated legal authority. The caliph had become an absolute ruler, ignoring the precepts of Islam that had been laid down by the first four rightly guided caliphs, all original converts of Muhammad. According to these principles, the caliph should be a member of the Quraysh tribe of Muhammad, be elected to office by a council of Muslim elders, and use his power to spread the message of Islam.

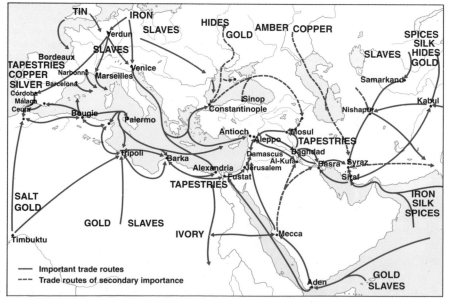

Two men prepare a medicine. Illustration from an Arab version of *De materia medica V libri* (*Five Books on Healing Substances*), a book on herbs from the first century AD written by the Greek doctor Dioscorides.

Trade contacts in the Islamic world (eighth to eleventh centuries)

## Baghdad

Al-Mansur, who consolidated Abassid power, was the brother and successor to Abū al-'Abbās, and no less a despot. Like many other kings, he wanted to found a splendid new capital. Initially he considered building his palace from the stones of the old Persian residence in the capital at Ctesiphon, but fortunately, it did not happen, and the unique monument was saved for posterity. Al-Mansur found an area on the banks of the Tigris where there were many Nestorian monasteries. (These dated from an era when the teachings of the Christian prelate Nestorius, declared a heretic in 431, had been popular.) In order to supervise the construction of his new city, Al-Mansur made his home in one of these monasteries.

The workmen began building at a designated area near the village of Baghdad. The new capital was to be completely circular.

Inside the round walls were the main palaces, offices, and mosques. The city developed into a nonresidential center of government. The market, which had been situated between the double outer walls, was relocated as well, because the caliph was constantly afraid of riots and preferred not to have crowds of easily aroused people so near him. The center of the city was even declared a sacred space, protected by law forbidding all mortals except the caliph from appearing there on horseback.

Around the palace then, the large, chaotic, noisy city of Baghdad was rapidly growing into the commercial center of the Muslim world. All of its wealth was displayed in the streets. Craftsmen worked in the open air. Huge masses of people congested the markets, buying and selling and transporting goods.

The presence of the caliph guaranteed

An eleventh-century sultan on horseback speaks to a woman; his followers are standing around him. Persian miniature from the fifteenth century prosperity for the people, but that did not guarantee his popularity. Baghdad had many discontented citizens. The Shiites were bitterly disappointed in the Abbasids, and during the night, there was much writing of graffiti. Many mornings, curses directed at Baghdad's ruler could be read on its walls. The caliph received such signs of opposition with great displeasure. Disrespect did not fit with his concept of authority and it was his

taries displayed on the bridge over the Tigris. People fantasized about the life of the caliph and tended to attribute the responsibility for tyranny and corruption to bad public servants who committed such crimes without the knowledge of the Ruler of the Believers. There was no real political consciousness, only at most, perhaps, disgust and sympathy. On occasion, popular resistance in Baghdad could go quite far. In clear daylight, Turkish soldiers were molested in the streets and those who dared enter the city at night rarely returned home.

For his own safety and that of the guardians of his throne, the caliph established a new capital at Samarra, where he created a more pleasant atmosphere. Samarra was only the capital of the caliphate for a few decades. After that, the Abbasids returned to Baghdad, which by then had ceased to be the center of the Arab world. The focus had shifted to Egypt and the Fatimid caliphs. In the tenth century they founded their capital, the new and glorious city of Cairo, near the old town of Fustat.

## Particularism

The capital of Islamic culture was relocated with some regularity, but seldom by chance. The Arab world was a large one, full of internal contradictions. The phenomenon of *particularism* was evident everywhere. This was the policy of allowing diverse cultures or peoples within the empire to function independently without regard for the whole. Particularism was not surprising, given that the Arabs had overpowered innumerable peoples. Despite the unifying influence of religion and language, regional differences continued to exist. Arabic dialects evolved to the extent that a person from the Maghreb could understand nothing an Iraqi said. However, the written language remained the same throughout the empire, from India to Spain. Modern observers are amazed at the extent of the unity that the Arabs, in spite of everything, managed to enjoy. Rarely has such a heterogeneous world been kept together for so long and with so much success.

Literary gathering in a garden in Baghdad. In the top half of the picture, a farmer drives his oxen, setting a waterwheel in motion so that the garden is constantly watered. Miniature from a thirteenth-century Arabian manuscript, *Makamat*, by al-Hariri

custom to immediately quash even the most minor resistance. He set up an army of spies to search out suspicious citizens.

Since the time of Al-Mansur, all caliphs had tended to act tyrannically, being increasingly intolerant of nonbelievers. The ruler of the faithful no longer had any contact with his subjects, living in elevated isolation. *Hajib*, the word which described his attendant, or chamberlain, literally meant something like curtain or room screen. This described the caliph's needs: The court was a hotbed of intrigue and a sensible emperor trusted no one. On the street, though, there was little evidence of this internal fight for favor, and people gazed in awe at the splendor of the court. They looked with some satisfaction at the heads of fallen court digni-

# TIME LINE

| THE WESTERN WORLD POLITICAL HISTORY | THE WESTERN WORLD CULTURAL HISTORY | EVENTS IN THE REST OF THE WORLD |
|---|---|---|
| **285–305** The emperor Diocletian creates a tetrarchy, two *caesars* (emperors) and their *augusti* (vice emperors); reforms government | **285–305** *Dominus et deus*, the emperor is both secular ruler and God; increasing numbers of civil servants and soldiers with rising taxes as a result; professions become hereditary | **c. 300** Advanced civilization among the Mayans; first Japanese invasion of Korea |
| **305** Diocletian resigns | | **306** Rise of the Chin dynasty in the east of China |
| **306** Constantius, ruler of the Western Empire, dies; army proclaims his son Constantine as successor | | **309-379** Shapur II, a Persian king, conquers large parts of eastern Syria |
| **312** Constantine defeats his rival Maxentius at the Milvian Bridge | | |
| **313** Edict of Milan proclaims the Christian Church a legal entity | | |
| | | **320-499** The north of India is ruled by the Gupta dynasty |
| **324** Constantine is the sole ruler of the Roman Empire | **324–330** Foundation of the new capital Constantinople (Roma Nova), settled by the Christian elite and immigrants; crossroads of East and West, with Greek the common language | |
| **330** Constantine founds a new imperial capital at Byzantium, renaming it Constantinople; also called *Roma Nova* (New Rome) | **324–337** Construction of the Augustium in Constantinople, introduction of horse races | |
| | **325** Arians branded heretics at the first council of Nicaea | |
| **337** Death of Constantine the Great | **337–361** The new emperor Constantius II is a follower of Arianism | |
| **c. 337–340** Constantius II seizes power | | |
| | | **350** Buddhism penetrates China as far as the imperial court |
| **361–363** Julian the Apostate reintroduces ancient Roman traditions and tries to repress Christianity for a short time | **361–363** Temporary restoration of the ancient pagan religion; copper money with fixed value is used | |
| **363** Jovian, a Christian officer, is proclaimed emperor by the army | | |
| **364** Valentinian I; the empire suffers from Diocletian's rigid legislation | | |
| **367–383** Gratian reigns as emperor | | |

| Prehistory | Antiquity | Middle Ages | Renaissance | Modern History | Contemporary History |
|---|---|---|---|---|---|

| THE WESTERN WORLD POLITICAL HISTORY | THE WESTERN WORLD CULTURAL HISTORY | EVENTS IN THE REST OF THE WORLD |
|---|---|---|
| **370** | | |
| **375** 375 Huns destroy the empire of the Ostrogoths <br> 375–378 Valens becomes emperor <br> 378 Battle of Adrianople; the Goths conquer and reign supreme in the Balkans <br> **380** 379 Theodosius I is coemperor in the East <br> 382 Under a negotiated peace, the Goths are allowed to live by their own laws south of the Danube <br> 383 Gratian is succeeded as emperor by Valentinian II; **385** actual power is in the hands of Theodosius | c. 375–500 The Great Migration causes the native populations of Europe to be dominated by immigration from the East <br> 379–395 Depopulation and impoverishment; Christianity becomes the state religion of the empire | 375–414 Chandragupta II creates a golden age in India <br><br> |
| **390** | | |
| **395** 395 After Theodosius's death the definitive division of the Roman Empire into an eastern and a western part takes place under his two sons <br> 395 Major revolt by the Visigoths; they advance southward and settle for a while in Epirus, Greece <br> 395–400 Eutropius becomes chamberlain to the young emperor Arcadius <br> **400** c. 400–500 Power among the Teutons shifts from popular assembly to king; a court chancellor is appointed <br> 400 Gainas the Goth has great power in Constantinople's government <br> **405** 401–403 Led by Alaric, the Visigoths invade Italy and are defeated by Stilicho <br> 408 Stilicho is killed; Theodosius II succeeds his father Arcadius as emperor of the Eastern Roman Empire <br> **410** 409 The Vandals and Suevi reach Spain <br> 410 Rome plundered by the Goths; death of Alaric <br> 410–415 Ataulf attempts to create a kingdom in southern Gaul but is driven off to Spain | 400–600 Theological disputes about Christ's divinity; opposition between Monophysites and orthodox Christians | c. 400 The Yamato Empire in Japan <br><br> |
| **415** | | |
| 418 The Visigoths as *foederati* are granted residence in Aquitaine in return for military service; **420** they found the kingdom of Toulouse | | |
| **425** | | |
| **430** 429 Vandals leave Spain and cross the Strait of Gibraltar into North Africa <br> 431 Fourth Council of Chalcedon declares Christ the Savior to be both human and divine | 430 Theodosius II erects new walls around Constantinople | |
| **435** 439 The Vandals conquer Carthage <br> **440** 440–461 Pope Leo I (the Great) <br> 441–453 Attila is ruler of the Huns <br> 442 The emperor recognizes the independent kingdom of the Vandals | | |
| **445** | | |
| **450** c. 450 The Huns invade the West; General Aëtius holds actual power in Rome. He then concludes an alliance with the Visigoths against the Huns <br> 450 Marcian is elected emperor in Constantinople, grants land to the Ostrogoths in Pannonia <br> 451 Battle on the Catalaunian Plain (in present-day France); the Huns are defeated; Aëtius allows them to depart without pursuit <br> 452 Attila invades the Po River Valley in Italy, but does not advance as far as Rome <br> 453 Death of Attila; the Huns are no longer a significant power <br> 454 Death of Aëtius; the emperor Valentinian is murdered | | |

| Prehistory | Antiquity | Middle Ages | Renaissance | Modern History | Contemporary History |
|---|---|---|---|---|---|

| THE WESTERN WORLD POLITICAL HISTORY | THE WESTERN WORLD CULTURAL HISTORY | EVENTS IN THE REST OF THE WORLD |
|---|---|---|
| 455 Vandals invade Italy and plunder Rome | | |
| 474–491 Zeno is emperor | | |
| 476 The last western emperor is deposed by Odoacer; he sends the imperial insignia to Constantinople | | |
| 481 Death of Childeric, who is succeeded by Clovis as king of the Franks | | |
| 483 Theodoric unites the Ostrogoths | | |
| 488 Theodoric leads the Ostrogoths against Italy | | |
| 491–518 Anastasius, ruler of the Byzantine Empire, is a follower of the Monophysites | | |
| 493 Theodoric murders Odoacer and his followers | 493–526 Under Theodoric, revival of Latin culture in Italy; scholars Cassiodorus and Boethius work at his court | |
| 493–526 Theodoric the Great | | |
| 496 Clovis defeats the army of the Alemanni and is baptized as a Christian in Reims | 496 Many Frankish nobles convert to Christianity, following the lead of their ruler, Clovis | 500–600 *Kama Sutra* written in India |
| 507 Clovis drives the Visigoths beyond the Pyrenees | c. 500–600 The languages of the Germanic peoples disappear; Latin continues as the written language; the circulation of money comes to a halt; Roman monuments become sources of materials for new buildings | |
| 511 Death of Clovis | | |
| 512 Uprising in Constantinople against the emperor Anastasius | | |
| 518-527 Justin rules the Eastern Roman Empire | | |
| 527–565 The emperor Justinian tries to control both factions in Constantinople, and also attempts to restore the Roman Empire; the empress Theodora has great influence | | 525 The White Huns are driven out of India |
| | | 529 Plato's Academia in Athens is closed |
| 532 Nika riot in Constantinople; a revolt against the emperor Justinian is suppressed in a massacre | 534 Completion of the *Corpus Juris Civilis* under the leadership of the jurist Tribonian | 532 Persian power extends to the Caucasus; Eternal Peace under the emperor Justinian |
| 535 The Byzantine Empire conquers part of North Africa and Sicily | 537 Completion of *Hagia Sophia* (Church of the Holy Wisom) in Constantinople | |
| 547 Death of the empress Theodora | | |
| 550 Byzantines conquer the coastal area of southern Spain | c. 550 Both Visigoths and Burgundians convert to the Christian faith | |
| | | 552 Monks introduce Buddhism in Japan |
| | 562 Completion of the new dome of *Hagia Sophia* | |
| 565 Byzantines have great difficulty controlling the conquered regions | | |
| 568 The Avars drive the Lombards toward Italy | | |
| | | c. 570 Birth of the prophet |

| Prehistory | Antiquity | Middle Ages | Renaissance | Modern History | Contemporary History |
|---|---|---|---|---|---|

| | THE PERSIAN EMPIRE POLITICAL HISTORY | THE PERSIAN EMPIRE CULTURAL HISTORY | EVENTS IN THE REST OF THE WORLD |
|---|---|---|---|
| 110 | | | |
| 135 | 114–117 The emperor Trajan defeats the Parthians | | |
| 160 | | | |
| 185 | 162–165 Lucius Verus defeats the Parthians<br>197–199 Parthians again defeated by the emperor Septimius Severus | | |
| 210 | | | |
| 235 | 226 Ardashir, governor of the province of Persia, ascends the throne of the last Parthian king Artabanus; beginning of the Sassanid dynasty<br>242-272 Shapur is king of the Persians | 226 Promotion of the cult of fire and worship of Ahura Mazda<br><br>242–272 Compilation of the *Zend Avesta*; strengthening of the state religion during a period of eclecticism and a strong expansion of Buddhism; rise of the new religion of the Manichaeans | |
| 260 | 260 The emperor Valerian suffers a devastating defeat by the Persian army | 260 Influence of Christianity in the New Persian Empire | |
| 285 | | | 285–305 Diocletian and the tetrarchy rule the Roman Empire |
| 310 | 302 Ormuz is king of the Persian Empire; creation of special courts protecting the poor against abuse<br>309–379 Shapur II conquers large parts of eastern Syria | | 306 Rise of the Chin dynasty in eastern China<br>320–499 Beginning of the Gupta dynasty in India |
| 335 | 363 Julian, the Western Roman emperor, dies in battle during an expedition against the Persians<br>379 The Persian Empire is at the zenith of its power | | 324–337 Constantine the Great is the sole ruler of the Roman Empire<br>361–363 Julian the Apostate |
| 360 | | | |
| 385 | | | |
| 410 | | | 410 Plunder of Rome by Alaric |
| 435 | | | 439 The Vandals conquer Carthage |
| 460 | | c. 450 Increasing importance of Christianity; most Christians in the Persian Empire are followers of the Nestorian Church | |
| 485 | | | |
| 510 | | | 500–600 *Kama Sutra* in India<br>511 Death of Clovis, king of the Franks |
| 535 | 531 Khosrow, "Splendid fame," ascends the Persian throne<br>532 Eternal Peace under the emperor Justinian, Khosrow expands the Persian Empire to the Caucasus | | 525 The White Huns are driven from India<br>532 Nika revolt in Constantinople |
| 560 | | c. 550 Khosrow raises a professional army; construction of dikes and canals; science and philosophy flourish at his court | 534 Completion of the *Corpus Juris Civilis* |
| 585 | 590–628 King Khosrow II | | |
| 610 | 613 Victory of the Persians over the Byzantines at Antioch; Syria becomes a Persian province<br>614 Persians occupy Jerusalem<br>622 A Persian attack in the direction of Constantinople fails; the emperor Heraclius campaigns in Armenia<br>627 Khosrow II is defeated by Heraclius at Nineveh<br>628 Death of Khosrow II; peace with the Byzantines | | 610–640 Emperor Heraclius of Byzantium |
| 635 | | | 632 Death of the prophet Muhammad |
| 660 | c. 650 Definitive end of the Sassanid Empire | c. 650 *Book of the Heroic Deeds of Ardashir* | |
| 1000 | | c. 1000 Flowering of Persian poetry with the poet Firdawsī, *Shah-nama* (*The Book of Kings*) | |

| Prehistory | Antiquity | Middle Ages | Renaissance | Modern History | Contemporary History |
|---|---|---|---|---|---|

| ISLAM POLITICAL HISTORY | ISLAM CULTURAL HISTORY | EVENTS IN THE REST OF THE WORLD |
|---|---|---|

**570** — 570 Birth of the prophet Muhammad in Mecca

**575** — 575 After staying with the Bedouin, Muhammad returns to his ancestral home

**580** — 579 Muhammad moves to the house of his uncle

**585** —

**590** — 589 Construction of the Great Canal in China

590–628 Khosrow II king of the Persians

**595** — 595 Muhammad marries his employer Khadija

**600** — c. 600 Recording of the prophecies of Muhammad; "Allah is the only god and Muhammad is his prophet"

**605** —

**610** — 610–641 Heraclius is emperor of the Byzantines

613–628 Battle between the Byzantines and the Persians

**615** —

**620** — 619 Muhammad and his followers live as exiles in Mecca

622 Muhammad and his followers leave for Medina

**625** —

628 Treaty with Mecca, the followers of Muhammad gain free passage to the Kaaba

629 First pilgrimage to Mecca

**630** — 630 Muhammad returns to Mecca; the Kaaba becomes the center of the new teachings

631 At Muhammad's instigation the followers of other religions are persecuted

632 Death of Muhammad, Abū Bakr becomes the first caliph

632–634 Abū Bakr defeats his domestic enemies and advances against Syria and Persia; beginning of the jihad, the "Holy War"

632 Almost all Arabs have become Muslim

632–680 Expansion of Islam

**635** — 634–644 Omar is the new caliph

636 Conquest of Damascus

637 Fall of the Persian capital of Ctesiphon

639 The Arabs invade Egypt

636 Islam is not imposed on new subjects

**640** — 641 The Arabs conquer Alexandria

642 Construction of Arab army camps in conquered territory

641 The library of Alexandria is destroyed by a fire

644 Death of Omar, who is succeeded by Othman, a member of the old merchant aristocracy of Mecca; the opposition is led by Ali, Muhammad's son-in-law

**645** —

**650** —

**655** —

656 Death of Othman; Ali becomes the new caliph, but encounters great resistance

657 Battle of Siffin: battle between Ali and the Muʿāwiyā of the Umayyads; the battle is undecided

658 The arbitration court condemns both parties; civil war

656 Ali moves the residence to Al-Kufa

**660** — 661 Assaults on Ali and Muʿāwiyā, Ali dies; Ali's son Hussein transfers the caliphate to Muʿāwiyā; beginning of the Umayyad dynasty

661 Rise of the Shiites who defend Ali's right to rule the Islamites; Damascus becomes the new residence, Medina becomes a pilgrimage site

| Prehistory | Antiquity | Middle Ages | Renaissance | Modern History | Contemporary History |
|---|---|---|---|---|---|

| | ISLAM POLITICAL HISTORY | ISLAM CULTURAL HISTORY | EVENTS IN THE REST OF THE WORLD |
|---|---|---|---|
| 660 | 661–680 Mu'āwiyā rules from Damascus with the assistance of court favorites; corruption and intrigues flourish at the secular court | 661–750 Flourishing of Islamic poetry and arts; conversion of the Basilica of St. John in Damascus into a mosque; flourishing of trade and industry in Damascus | |
| 665 | | | |
| 670 | 661–750 Opposition to the government by Shiites and converts | | |
| | 674–679 The Arabs besiege Constantinople | | |
| 680 | 680 Mu'āwiyā is succeeded by his son Yazīd'I; Ali's son Hussein claims the caliphate and is killed | | |
| 690 | | | |
| | 698 The Arabs conquer Carthage and reach the Atlantic Ocean | | |
| 700 | | | |
| 710 | 711 Tarik crosses the Strait of Gibraltar and conquers the empire of the Visigoths | | |
| 720 | 712 Arabian Bedouin armies reach the Indus; conquest of Turkestan | | 714–741 Charles Martel becomes court chancellor of the Frankish Empire |
| | 717 Constantinople besieged again, but quickly released | | 717 Power in Constantinople is in the hands of the Aetolian general Leo |
| 730 | | | |
| 740 | 732 Battle of Poitiers, Charles Martel halts the advance of the Muslim army which withdraws behind the Pyrenees | | |
| | 746 All of Persia revolts under the leadership of Abu Muslim | | |
| 750 | 750 Death of the last Umayyad caliph; dynasty of the Abbasids | | |
| 760 | 750–754 Caliph Abū al-'Abbās | | |
| 770 | 754–775 Caliph Al-Mansur includes new converts in the government and employs a policy of reconciliation | 754–775 In Iraq, the new capital, Baghdad, the "City of Peace," is built and becomes the center of trade, industry, and culture; poets praise the deeds of the great caliph | |
| 780 | 756 Abd ar-Rahmōn founds the emirate of Córdoba in Spain | | |
| 790 | 786–809 Caliph Harun Al-Rashid; the caliphate of the Abbasids experiences a golden age | | |
| 800 | | 800–1000 Arab trade and commerce reach their zenith | 800 Charlemagne is crowned emperor |
| | 809–850 Caliph al-Mamun | | 802–812 Nicephorus is emperor |
| 825 | | c. 825 The sect of the Sunnites is persecuted by Al-Mamun; golden age for science and the arts | 822 Revolt under Thomas the Slav causes unrest in the Byzantine Empire |
| 850 | c. 850 Disintegration of the empire, revolts and civil war, rise of small principalities | | 855 The Vikings sack Paris |
| 875 | | | |
| 900 | c. 900–1000 Beginning of the Reconquista, the recovery of Muslim territory throughout Spain | | |
| 925 | 929 The Caliphate of Córdoba is proclaimed | | 919 Henry the Fowler on the German throne |
| 950 | 945 The office of Prince of Princes falls to a Shiite family | | 955 The Frankish king Otto I defeats the Magyars at Lechfield |
| 975 | 969–1171 The caliphate of the Fatimids | 969 Cairo founded by the Fatimids | 960–1279 Sung dynasty in China |
| 1000 | c. 1000–1200 Seljuks rule Baghdad | 969–1171 Trade with China and India produces great prosperity in the Fatimid Empire | 1001 Muslims occupy the Punjab |
| 1025 | 1025 End of the Caliphate of Córdoba | | |
| 1050 | | | 1031–1260 Spanish *Reconquista* |
| 1075 | | | |
| 1100 | | | 1080 Conquest of Toledo by the Christians |
| 1150 | | | 1094 El Cid conquers Valencia from the Muslims |
| | | | 1181 Francis of Assisi in Italy |
| 1200 | c. 1200 The Christians reconquer most of Spain | | 1185 First shogunate in Japan |
| | | | 1206 Rise of the Mongol Empire under Genghis Khan |
| 1250 | 1256 Mongols invade Persia | | |
| 1300 | 1260 Baghdad destroyed by the Mongols | | |
| | | | 1469 The Catholic rulers, Ferdinand and Isabella, are married in Spain |
| 1400 | 1492 The Catholic kings of Spain conquer Granada | | |

| Prehistory | Antiquity | Middle Ages | Renaissance | Modern History | Contemporary History |
|---|---|---|---|---|---|

# Glossary

**Abbasids** dynasty of caliphs formed by descendants of Muhammad's uncle Abbas; ruled from Baghdad (750–1258) until it was sacked by Mongols. Accorded purely religious function in Egypt, Abbasids held power there from 1261 to 1517.

**Abū al-'Abbās** first *caliph* (successor) of the Abbasid dynasty (750–754); gained power through the influence of Shiite Abū Muslim but actually opposed and persecuted Shiites.

**Abū Bakr** first leader of Islam after the death of Muhammad (632–634); took the Arabic title *khalifat Rasul Allah* (successor to the Messenger of God); father-in-law and first convert made by Muhammad outside his own family; began *Jihad* (Holy War), seizing Syrian territory from the Persians.

**Abū Muslim** (died 754) Persian Shiite Muslim who undermined Muslim popular support for the Umayyad dynasty in favor of the first Abbasid caliph Abū al-'Abbās; supported Abbasid Al Mansūr's claim to the throne but was later murdered by him.

**Achaemenids** dynasty that ruled Persia (550 BC–330 BC).

**Ahura Mazda** Zoroastrian god of light and truth.

**Aisha or Ayeshah** (c.614–678) devoted second wife of the Prophet Muhammad, following the death of his first wife, Khadija; daughter of Muhammad's adviser and eventual successor, Abū Bakr; called the Mother of the Believers.

**Al Mansūr** caliph of the Abbasid dynasty (754); founder of Baghdad; attempted to unify the realm through religion; accorded equal rights to all Muslim men.

**Alaric I** (c.370–c.410) king of the Visigoths (395–410); led Visigoths employed by Roman Emperor Theodosius (394); declared king by them after Theodosius's death (395); invaded Corinth, Argos, and Sparta, accepted ransom from Athens in lieu of sacking it; defeated by Roman General Flavius Stilicho; made prefect of Illyricum; invaded Italy and was defeated by Stilicho (402); besieged Rome, was paid ransom, but sacked the city anyway (410).

**Alemanni** southern Germanic people; threatened Roman borders and invaded Gaul in the third century AD; conquered eastern Gaul at the end of the fourth century; defeated by Frankish King Clovis I.

**Ali of Arabia or Ali ibn Abi Talib** (died 661) son-in-law of Muhammad, made fourth caliph of Islam (656). His rule was disputed by Mu'āwiyah I, kinsman of Uthman, who succeeded him. Ali was assassinated by his own deserting followers, the Kharijites, in 661.

**Allah** Arabic word for God.

**Anastasius I** (c.430–518) Byzantine emperor (491–518); supporter of Monophysite doctrine; in 512, built the Anastasius Wall west of Constantinople.

**Angles** Germanic people; settled in eastern England in the fifth century AD.

**Arabia** desert peninsula lying between the Mediterranean Sea on the east, the Persian Gulf on the north, and the Red Sea on the south; populated by Bedouin people; most of the populace converted to Islam about 630.

**Arabic crafts** included woven cloth from Damascus and Mosul (damask and muslin), Spanish wrought ironwork, and Persian and Armenian hand-knotted carpets.

**Arcadius** (c.337–408) son of Roman Emperor Theodosius I; Eastern Roman emperor in Constantinople at age eighteen.

**Ardashir I** king of Persia (224–241).

**Arianism** doctrine of theologian Arius (fourth century); held that Jesus Christ was not of the same substance as God, but merely the best of created beings.

**Artabanus V** king of Parthia (213–224).

**Ataulf** Visigoth king (410–415).

**Attila** (c.406–453) king of the Huns (c.433–453); conquered Western Europe; defeated in Gaul by a coalition of Romans and Visigoths (451); plundered Italy (452).

**Baghdad** (Syria) residence of the Abbasid caliphs, built by Al-Mansūr to appease the Persian Muslims; center of trade, industry, and Persian culture; destroyed by Mongols.

**Battle of Adrianople** (Turkey) 20,000 Visigoths defeated and killed Roman Emperor Valens and most of his troops in 378.

**Battle of the Milvian Bridge** (312) near Rome; victory of Constantine over his Italian rival, Maxentius.

**Bedouin** nomad people of the Arabian desert; converted to Islam about 622; dominated non-Islamic population under the Umayyads; forced to yield power to the Abbasid dynasty (c.750).

**Belisarius** (sixth century) general of Emperor Justinian; conquered the Vandal kingdom in North Africa (533–534); defeated the Ostrogoths in Italy (540).

**Bleda** (died 445) nephew of Hun king Roas who succeeded him with his brother Attila; murdered by Attila.

**Blues** political party in Constantinople that organized important horse races against the Greens. Despite the lack of a clear political program, they had great influence on politics and religion.

**Boeotia** (480–524) Roman philosopher and statesman; Theodoric's political advisor; executed for high treason. His work on Greek scientific philosophers, notably Aristotle, had great influence on medieval scholastics.

**Byzantine Empire** eastern part of the Roman Empire that survived the disintegration of the Western Empire in the fifth century AD; named for the former capital city Byzantium (renamed Constantinople, now Istanbul); eastern Roman provinces included southeastern Europe and the Balkan Peninsula, southwestern Asia and the Middle East (modern Syria, Jordan, Israel, Lebanon, and Cyprus), and northeast Africa (Egypt and eastern Libya); war with Persians, Arabs, and Turks reduced the empire to Asia Minor and the Balkans; conquered by the Turks in 1453.

**Cairo** (Egypt) capital of the anticaliphate of the Fatimids; founded in 969; became an important metropolis that took over trade with India and China from Baghdad.

**caliph** (from *khalifah*, Arabic: successor) religious and political leader of Islam; successor to Muhammad. Competing caliphs divided the Islamic states.

**caliphate** office and realm held by a caliph.

**Caliphate of Córdoba** Islamic state in Spain founded by Umayyad Abd al Rāhmōn (c.750); proclaimed a caliphate (929).

**capitation** tax in fixed amount payable by all adult men subjected by Muslims; imposed in addition to tax on landholdings. By the end of the seventh century, many men converted to Islam in order to avoid taxation.

**caravans** desert convoys using camels as pack animals to transport trade products from Arabia.

**Cassiodorus** (c.490–583) Roman statesman and scholar; held high ministerial posts in the service of Theodoric; author of theological and literary textbooks; stimulated the copying of manuscripts in monasteries.

**Châlons-sur-Marne** site of massive battle between Romans, assisted by Visigoths, and Attila the Hun in 451; Attila's defeat.

**Charles Martel** (the Hammer) (c.688–741) Carolingian Frankish *majordomo* (mayor of the palace) and ruler of Austrasia (modern northeastern France, southwestern Germany) (715–741); son of Pépin of Herstal; grandfather of Charlemagne; battled Alemanni, Bavarians, and Saxons; defeated an Islamic army near Poitiers in 732, preventing the Muslim conquest of Europe.

**cheques** (Arabic: bills) bonds used in lieu of currency, widely accepted in trading and banking centers like Baghdad and Córdoba.

**Clotilda** (470–545) daughter of Chilperic, king of Burgundy; married Clovis I (493); influential in his conversion to Christianity; canonized (c.549).

**Clovis I** (c.466–511) king of the Franks (481–511); conquered Gaul, except for Brittany and the south coast; defeated Alemanni and Visigoths; baptized in 496.

**Constantine the Great, Flavius Valerius Constantinus** (c.274–337) Roman emperor (306–337); initially emperor in the West, became absolute sovereign in 323; built Constantinople; legalized Christianity.

**Constantinople** (now Istanbul) founded by Constantine I in 324 as capital of the Byzantine (Eastern Roman) Empire and imperial residence; lying on both sides of the Bosporus Strait, separating Europe from Asia.

***Corpus Iuris Civilis*** (Latin: *Body of Civil Law*) civil code composed by order of Emperor Justinian I under supervision of jurist Tribonian in the sixth century; classified and corrected all

Roman jurisprudence to that time; referred to as the Justinian Code.

**Council of Nicaea** (325) convoked by Constantine I; defined Christian doctrine.

**Council of Dad-Ishu** (424) formally separated Eastern Christian church from Western.

**Ctesiphon** capital of Persian Empire.

**Damascus** ancient city in Syria; residence of Umayyad dynasty (661–746); center of Arab culture and trade, famous for damask.

**Diocletian, Gaius Aurelius Valerius Dioclectianus** (245–313) Roman emperor (284–305); last of the Illyrian dynasty; modernized administrative and military organization; established tetrarchy; divided the empire east and west; organized tax reforms and price controls.

*dirham* coin used in Constantinople.

**dominate** Roman imperial era starting with Diocletian, in which emperors were absolute rulers and the state was despotic, with compelled hereditary succession and increasing bureaucracy. Constantinople became the new government center, Christianity became more and more important, and the pressure on the borders increased.

*Du'a* (Arabic: private prayer) prayer used in Islam.

**Eastern Empire** eastern part of the Roman Empire, divided after the death of Theodosius in 395. About the sixth century, it was called the Byzantine Empire, with Constantinople as its capital.

**Edict of Milan** (313) proclaimed by Constantine the Great with his coemperor, Licinius, legalizing Christian worship.

**Ephthalites** also called White Huns; defeated Persian King Firuz II in 431.

**Ermanaric** fourth-century Gothic king; founded a kingdom from the Baltic Sea to the Black Sea.

**eunuchs** castrated men who often managed palace administration and became influential confidants of emperors.

**Fatimids** Shiite dynasty of caliphs in North Africa (909–1177); descended from Muhammad's daughter Fatima; conquered Egypt and founded Cairo (c.950).

**Firdawsi, Abdul Kasim Hasan** Persian poet who wrote *Shah-nama* (*Book of Kings*) (c.1000).

**Five Pillars of Islam** confession of faith, prayer, almsgiving, fasting, and pilgrimage.

*foederati* (Latin: the federated) foreigners allied with the Romans; populated and patrolled land at imperial borders; provided troops for the Roman army.

**Franks** Germanic people who established themselves as *foederati* (allies) along the Rhine River over the third century AD; divided into two main groups, Ripuarian Franks on the middle section of the river, and the Salian Franks on its lower reaches; led by Clovis I, conquered

territory between the Rhine and the Pyrenees Mountains, including Syagrius's Roman kingdom in Gaul (end of the fifth century); forced the Visigoths to Spain (507).

**Gainas** (died 400) Gothic mercenary general; appropriated power in Constantinople with his army; hated by the populace, especially because of his Arian beliefs; died in rebellion against him.

**Gaiseric** (c.400–477) king of the Vandals (428–477).

**Gallia Placidia** sister of Western Roman Emperor Honorius; taken hostage by Alaric I when he plundered Rome in 410.

*Germania* (Latin: *Germany*) written AD 98 by Roman Cornelius Tacitus; commentary on Germanic people.

**Germanic kings** Germanic commanders in chief, initially chosen by tribesmen, who gained power with increased territory, becoming absolute rulers.

**Germanic kingdoms** in Europe beginning in the fifth century; ruled by Germans who let popular customs continue; influenced by Roman culture.

**Gratian** (359–383) Western Roman emperor (367–383).

**Great Migration** that of the Germanic peoples to the south and the west of Europe between the fourth and the sixth centuries AD; one of the causes of the decline of the Western Roman Empire in 476.

**Greek fire** secret Byzantine weapon, used especially against Arabs at sieges of Constantinople (674, 680, 717); the substance burned spontaneously when sprayed onto enemy ships; almost unquenchable.

**Greens** party in Constantinople influential in politics and religion; organized horse races against the Blues party; comprised traders and working-class people.

*Hadith* (Arabic: *Story*); companion book to the Koran; guide for Muslim daily life; details incidents in Muhammad's life, his particular preferences and maxims.

**Hagar** biblical second wife of Abraham, mother of Ismael.

**Hagia Sophia** great domed Church of the Holy Wisdom in Constantinople; built under Emperor Justinian (532–537).

*hajj* (Arabic: pilgrimage) journey to Mecca.

**Harun ar-Rashid** caliph (786–809); under him, the caliphate of the Abbasids reached its peak.

*hegira* (Arabic: flight) journey of Muhammad from Mecca to Medina, September 20, 622; used as the first date of the Muslim calendar; considered the starting point of Islam.

**Heraclius** Byzantine emperor (610–641); began counteroffensive against Khosrow II (622); weakened the Persian Empire by his victories in the center of the realm (627).

*hicma* scientific center with a library built in

Baghdad by order of Abbasid caliph Al Mamun; he had his scientists study Greek culture and science; collected manuscripts.

**Honorius** (384–423) son of Roman Emperor Theodosious I; Western Roman emperor at age twelve (395–423), under the guardianship of Stilicho.

*hospitium* (Latin: guest right; English: hospice) Roman and foederati custom that carried obligations on the part of both guest and host; eventually became a euphemism for landowners to provide housing to foreign soldiers; practice of claiming a third of land settled (sometimes resolved through taxation); adopted by Germanic rulers to establish large kingdoms.

**Huns** central Asiatic people noted for horsemanship and ferocity in battle; drove the Visigoths from the Ukraine (c.370); conquered eastern and central Europe in the fifth century; seized western Europe under Attila (c.450).

**Hussein** (Husayn) son of Ali of Arabia; claimed the caliphate in Al-Kufa in 680; he and his clan were murdered by Umayyad armies of orthodox Muslims (Sunnites); adherents of Ali, called Shiites, seceded; his murder is commemorated annually.

*imam* (Arabic: predecessor) term used to designate Islamic priests or holy men. Shiites believe that a series of twelve imams, descended from Ali and Fatima, had the right to the leadership of the Muslims. According to their belief, the last imam disappeared, to return at the end of the world.

*insulae* (Latin: islands) Roman public apartment houses.

**Isaurians** mountain tribe from southern Asia Minor noted for military prowess; established a Byzantine imperial dynasty.

**Ishmael** biblical son of patriarch Abraham; progenitor of the Arabs.

**Islam** monotheistic religion worshiping Allah; founded by the Prophet Muhammad in the seventh century; its tenets, as revealed to him, are recorded in the Koran.

**Islamic Empire** expanded out of Arabia in the seventh and eighth centuries to Syria, Egypt, North Africa, Spain, and Asia to the Chinese border; despite religious unification, it did not become a single cultural entity; rebellions and relocations of power took place frequently.

**Jews in Medina** Jewish community in Arabian town of Medina; rejected religion and politics of Muhammad; allowed to keep their faith, but obliged to pay capitation and recognize Islam.

*jihad* (Arabic: Holy War) Muslim duty to expand Allah's realm, to propagate Islam; led to the conquering of Mesopotamia, Syria, Egypt, North Africa, Central Asia, and Spain in the seventh and eighth centuries.

**Jovian** (c.331–c.364) Roman emperor 363–364.

**Julian the Apostate** (c.331–363) Roman emperor (361–363); sought to restore Roman traditions and greatness; limited the rights of Christians; rid the army of non-Roman influences.

**Justinian I the Great, Flavius Petrus Sabgatius Justinianus** (483–565) Byzantine emperor (527–565); had the *Corpus Iuris Civilis* drawn up; built the great Hagia Sophia (Church of the Holy Wisdom). Under his policy of imperial renovation, he expanded Byzantine control of the West; recaptured North Africa, Italy, and the Spanish south coast; his generals Belisarius and Narses defeated the Ostrogoths.

*kampfio* Germanic ritual duel; used to prove the veracity of an accusation of witchcraft or prostitution.

*Kaaba* (Arabic: cube) black stone cube in Mecca originally considered holy by most Arabs for its more than 300 statues. Muhammad considered it a religious relic of Allah built by Ishmael and condemned the polytheism. Although driven away in 622, he returned to purge it in 628, making it the central temple of Islam.

**Khadija** (sixth century) first wife of Muhammad; a widow made wealthy through caravan trade. Their marriage enabled Muhammad to become a rich trader with ample time for mysticism and religion.

**Kharijites** followers of Ali of Arabia who deserted him in 657 after his agreement to arbitrate his dispute over the caliphate with rival Mu'āwiyah. This followed the inconclusive battle at Siffin (in northern Syria). Vowing to kill both, the Kharijites assassinated only Ali in 661.

**Khosrow I** (528–579) king of Persia (531–579); established a professional army; established a water supply; supported the poor and orphans; made his palace a center of philosophy, primarily Indian.

**Khosrow II** (died 628) king of Persia (590–628); seized Syria and Jerusalem from the Byzantines (613–614); continued conquest as far as Asia Minor and Egypt; defeated by Heraclius in 627.

**Koran** scripture of Islam, regarded by the faithful as revealed to Muhammad over twenty-two years and recorded by scribes; written in verses organized into 114 chapters called *suras*; contains the history of Muhammad, references to the Bible, and principles of Islamic law.

**Leo the Isaurian** Byzantine emperor (717–740); gained the throne after several succession conflicts; withstood an Arab siege; made the Byzantine Empire a buffer against Islamic expansion.

**Lombards** central European Germanic people; conquered most of Italy in 568, leaving Byzantine rule only on the coast and in the south. This Lombard Empire was subjected by Charlemagne in the eighth century.

*majordomo* (Latin: mayor of the palace) originally organizer of the royal household in the Frankish kingdom; eventually housekeepers were made royal ministers with administrative power.

**Mamelukes** originally Turkish slaves hired as mercenaries by caliphs in Cairo to maintain order in the twelfth century; gained power in 1260; dominated Egypt until the beginning of the nineteenth century.

**Mani** (c.216–c.276) Persian prophet who founded Manichaeism. Mani considered himself the final prophet in a series that included Zoroaster, Buddha, and Jesus.

**Manichaeism** religion founded by Mani in Mesopotamia; combines elements of Christianity, Zoroastrianism, Buddhism, and others; postulates two competing principles of good (referred to as light, God, the human soul) and evil (seen as darkness, the devil, the human body); considered knowledge of light through his teachings and an ascetic way of life as the way to salvation. Manichaeans were persecuted by Persian kings and Roman emperors.

*mawali* (Arabic) term for non-Arabic converts to Islam.

**Mecca** Arabian caravan town; fled by Muhammad for Medina in 622 due to popular resistance to his crusade against polytheism; Mecca accepted Muhammad's authority in 628; geographical center of Islam.

**Medina** Arabian oasis town to which Muhammad fled in 622; originally named Yathrib; renamed *Madinat al-Nabi* (the city of the prophet) or Medina. Muhammad converted its already largely monotheistic Jewish population, becoming its theocratic leader. Medina waged war against Mecca until 628.

**Mésé** main street of Constantinople; crafts and commercial center of the Byzantine Empire; many of the city's poor slept between its colonnades at night.

**Middle Ages** period between AD 500 and 1500; characterized by cultural decline and the disappearance of money, trade, and cities. Large landowners on autonomic rural estates gained wealth and power through the institution of serfdom, binding workers to them economically. Intellectual matters were left largely to priests.

**Monophysitism** (from Greek *monos*: single and *physis*: nature) a fifth- and sixth-century doctrine that contended Jesus Christ had only a single nature, which was divine, not human. This conflicted with the orthodox doctrine that Christ was at once divine and human.

**mosque** Islamic place of prayer; worship meetings are held on Friday; first mosque was founded in Medina on a Friday, on the spot where Muhammad prayed for the first time.

**Mu'āwiyah** first Umayyad caliph (656–680); moved the capital of Islam from Medina to Damascus; opposed Ali and his followers; dominated Syria and Egypt. After Ali's death, he bought off Ali's son Hassan to become absolute sovereign of the Arabian Empire.

*muezzin* (Arabic: singer) summons Muslim believers to prayer five times a day; first muezzin was the black slave Bilal in Medina.

**Muhammad** (c.570–632) founder of Islam; Arab prophet from Mecca; introduced monotheistic Islam as a reaction to Arab polytheism.

*mundium* (Latin: possession) Germanic concept of a man's right of possession over his wife and any other women he had, his children, his slaves, and his freedmen. Under it, women had no civil rights; could not inherit or administer property without approval from their husbands, fathers, or eldest sons.

**Muslim calendar** counts the years from September 20, 622, date of Muhammad's *Hegira* or flight from Mecca to Medina.

**Muslims** worshipers of Allah; members of Islam.

**Narses** (sixth century) general of Emperor Justinian I; originally head of the palace guard; defeated the Ostrogoths (led by Totila), restoring Byzantine influence in Italy (552).

**Nestorianism** doctrine of Nestorius (382–451), archbishop of Constantinople (428–431); postulated that Jesus Christ acted as a single person but did not have conjoined divine and human natures, being purely human on earth and purely god in heaven. In consequence, contended that Mary could not be called Mother of God; she begot the man Jesus, while God begot his divine aspect. This doctrine gained followers, notably in the New Persian Kingdom, against the orthodox Christian belief that Christ has two distinct natures, divine and human, joined in both person and substance. In the fifth century, Nestorianism spread throughout the Byzantine Empire; declared heretical by the Council of Ephesus (431). The Nestorian church became powerful where it sought refuge in Persia, India, China, and Mongolia in early medieval times.

**New Persian Kingdom** governed by Sassanid dynasty, founded by Ardashir (226); conquered by Arabs (651); notable for coexistence of many religions, including Christianity, Nestorianism, and Manichaeism.

**Nicomedia** capital of Roman Emperor Diocletian in northwestern Asia Minor.

**Nika revolt** (January 13–18, 532) uprising in Constantinople of the Greens and the Blues, who turned the population against Justinian; the population appointed a new emperor and destroyed the city center; Theodora barely prevented Justinian from fleeing; Belisarius repressed the revolt with mercenaries.

**Odoacer** (435–493) Herulian Germanic general; deposed last Roman emperor in 476, ending the Western Roman Empire; had himself proclaimed king of the first Germanic realm in Italy.

**Omar or Umar I** second caliph (634–644) in Mecca; defeated Byzantines in Syria, Persians in Mesopotamia; conquered Egypt (641); introduced financial reforms of *zakat* (tax for the poor) and capitation (head tax).

**Ormuz** New Persian king (302–309); protected the poor against abuse of power by special protective courts; died in battle against the Bedouin.

**Ostrogoths** Germanic tribe from Ukraine, subjected by the Huns; migrated to Hungary in the fifth century; established a kingdom in Italy under Theodoric (493); defeated under Totila (552).

**Othman** (Uthman I ibn Affan) Muhammad's son-in-law; third calpih (644–656)); founded Umayyad dynasty, appointing his clan members to important positions.

**Parthia** kingdom founded about 250 BC, located in today's Iran and Afghanistan.

**Parthians** inhabitants of Parthia (modern Iran and Afghanistan) notable for horsemanship; 1143 regularly waged war with the Roman Empire; conquered by rebelling Persians who founded the New Persian Kingdom (226).

**Picts** ancient people of Great Britain, driven into Scotland by Romans and Britons.

**Prince of Princes** title of Baghdad official (not caliph) ruling Shiite-dominated Arab Empire (945–1050); Seljuks restored the caliphate.

**Ravenna** Italian seaport conquered by Theodoric (493); recaptured by the Byzantines (540); made the center of Byzantine territory in Italy; conquered by the Lombards (eighth century).

*reconquista* (Spanish: reconquest) Christian reconquering of occupied Spain from the Muslims (tenth to thirteenth centuries).

*renovatio imperii* (Latin: imperial renovation) Emperor Justinian's plan to restore Roman prestige and return the western provinces to Byzantine rule. He reconquered the south coast of Spain, Italy, and North Africa.

**Roas or Rugilas** (died c. 433) Hun king.

**Romance languages** any of the languages derived from vernacular or Low Latin; originating in the Germanic kingdoms, they developed into separate languages; include French, Spanish, Italian, Portuguese, Catalan, Provençal, and Romanian.

**Romulus Augustulus** last Western Roman emperor; deposed in 476.

*salah* (Arabic: ritual prayer) Islamic prayer to be performed, facing Mecca, five times daily.

**Sarah** biblical first wife of Isaac.

**Sassanids** dynasty of kings (226–651); captured Mesopotamia and East Syria from the Byzantines (fourth century); conquered Jerusalem (614); defeated by Alexius (628).

**Saxons** ancient people of northern Germany; conquered parts of England in the fifth and sixth centuries.

**Seljuks** Turks who named themselves after their deceased leader; captured Baghdad from the Shiites; established power in Persia (c.1050); conquered Asia Minor (1071); their kingdom disintegrated by the end of the twelfth century.

*Shah-nama (Book of Kings)* Persian epic poem composed by Firdawsī (c.1000); rich in historical detail.

**Shapur I** king of Persia (241–272); expanded the New Persian Kingdom to the Himalayas; conquered Armenia; defeated the Byzantines in Antioch, taking many Syrian prisoners of war; Christianity spread throughout his realm.

**Shapur II** king of Persia (309–379); captured parts of eastern Syria and Mesopotamia from the Eastern Roman Empire; defeated Julian (363); brought the New Persian Kingdom to its apex.

**Sharia** the religious and moral principles of Islam, considered law in Islamic states.

*sheikh* (Arabic: leader) leader of the Bedouin people; chosen to solve conflicts; did not have absolute power.

**Shiites** (from *shi'ah*, Arabic: partisan) supporters of Muhammad's son-in-law Ali; seceded from orthodox Islam after the murder of Hussein in 680; they venerate their leaders (imams) as divinely guided; believe that a series of twelve imams, descended from Ali and Fatima, have the right to Muslim leadership; hold that the last imam disappeared, to return at the end of the world.

**Stilicho, Flavius** (359–408) Roman general who acted as regent and power behind the throne of Western Roman Emperor Flavius Honorious; ambassador to Persia (383); married niece of Emperor Theodosius I, with whom he was appointed joint guardian of Honorius; had his daughter married to Honorius (398); made consul (400); battled Visigoth King Alaric I (401, 403); defended Italy against Germanic/Celtic invaders led by Radagaisus (405); executed by order of Honorius under suspicion that he wanted to make his own son emperor.

**Sunnites** (from *sunnah*, Arabic: custom or law) orthodox Muslims who follow the Sunna or body of Islamic custom.

**Tarik** (eighth century) African Berber Muslim general; occupied Gibraltar in 711; took Spain from the Visigoths; *Gibraltar* means Tarik's rock.

**tetrarchy** government by four joint rulers, introduced by Diocletian in 293; he divided power between two augusti, assisted by two caesars who were their successors.

**Theodora** (c.508–548) Byzantine empress (527–548); originally a dancer and an actress, became wife of Emperor Justinian I; had considerable influence over his policy, due in part to her Monophysite convictions; saved Justinian's position during the Nika revolt.

**Theodoric the Great** (c.454–526) Ostrogoth king (474–526); founded Ostrogoth Kingdom in Italy with the permission of the Eastern Roman Empire of Odoacer; tried to restore Western Roman Empire politically and militarily.

**Theodosius I**, the Great, Flavius Theodosius (c.346–395) Eastern Roman emperor (379–395); Western Roman emperor (394–395); made peace with the Visigoths; prohibited all religions but Christianity; last ruler of a united Roman Empire. After his death, it was divided east and west between Arcadius and Honorius.

**Totila** Ostrogoth king (541–552); initially successful in driving the Byzantines out of Italy; defeated by Emperor Justinian's General Narses (552).

**trial by ordeal** Germanic custom to let God decide the guilt of an accused party by subjecting him to punishments (fire, walking hot coals, and the like); those who remained unhurt were considered innocent.

**Turkestan** region and modern country in central Asia; conquered by Arabs (beginning of the eighth century); their expansion was halted by Chinese border armies.

**Turks** Asian peoples north of Persia who converted to Islam, but retained their own language and customs. Their leaders, sultans, became more and more powerful from the ninth century onward and limited the power of the caliphs to religious issues.

**Ulfilas** Christian bishop who translated the Bible into Gothic, enabling large-scale Gothic conversions to Christianity.

**Umayyad dynasty** dynasty of caliphs in Damascus from the Umayyad clan that dominated the Arab world, including non-Islamic population (c.661–750); engaged in power struggle with the Shiites; ousted by the Abbasids.

**Ummah** Arabic tribal brotherhood forged by Muhammad.

**Valens** (c.328–378) Eastern Roman emperor (364–378); offered Visigoths land south of the Danube River; made them *foederati* (allies). They revolted due to lack of food, killing Valens in battle.

**Valentinian I** (321–375) Western Roman emperor (364–375).

**Valentinian II** (371–392) Western Roman emperor (375–392).

**Valentinian III** (419–455) Western Roman emperor (425–455).

**Vandals** eastern Germanic people; migrated to Gaul and Spain at the beginning of the fifth century; under Geiserik, founded a kingdom in North Africa (429); plundered Rome (455); defeated by Emperor Justinian I (534).

**Visigoths** (Latin: *Visigothi* or noble Goths) Germanic people from the Ukraine, driven out by the Huns; settled south of the Danube as *foederati* (allies) of Rome; rebelled in 378; plundered Rome under Alaric (410); established a kingdom in Spain conquered by the Arabs (711).

**Wallia** Visigoth king (415–418).

*wergeld* (German: fine) under Germanic criminal law, required to be paid by the killer of a person or an animal. People and animals were assigned values, depending on importance. This arrangement ended the Germanic *faidas* (feuds).

**Western Roman Empire** western part of the Roman Empire divided after Theodosius's death in 395. With Rome as its capital, it remained in existence until 476, when the last emperor was deposed by Odoacer.

**Yathrib** Arabian city renamed *Madinat al-Nabi* (the city of the prophet) or Medina.

**Yazdegerd III** last Sassanid king of Persia (632–641).

**Yazid I** caliph (680–683); son and successor of Mu'āwiyah.

*zakat* income tax paid by Muslims, intended for poor relief and charity; one of the religious duties for the exaltation of Allah.

*Zend-Avesta* prayer books of Zoroastrianism.

**Zoroastrianism** traditional religion of Persians prior to conversion to Islam; founded by Zoroaster; posited competing spirits of good and evil.

# Bibliography

**The Fall of Rome**
Garnsey, P. D. A., and Saller, R. P. *The Roman Empire: Economy, Society and Culture.* London, 1987.
Heather, P. J. *Goths and Romans, 332–489.* Oxford, 1991.
Marasovic, J. *Diocletian's Palace.* Split, 1972.
Millar, F. *The Roman Empire and Its Neighbours.* London, 1957.
Starr, C. G. *The Roman Empire, 27 BC–AD 476: A Study in Survival.* Oxford, 1982.
Thompson, E. A. *The Goths in Spain.* Oxford, 1969.
Wells, C. M. *The Roman Empire.* London, 1984.
Williams, S. *Diocletian and the Roman Recovery.* London, 1985.

**The Changing Face of Europe**
Briggs, M. S. *Goths and Vandals: A Study of Destruction, Neglect and Preservation.* London, 1952.
Ferreiro, A. *The Visigoths in Gaul and Spain.* Leiden, 1988.
Holmqvist, W. *German Art during the First Millennium AD.* Stockholm, 1955.
Kurth, G. *Clovis.* Brussels, 1929.
Murray, A. C. *Germanic Kinship Structure: Studies in Law and Society in Antiquity and the Early Middle Ages.* Toronto, 1983.
Owen, F. *The Germanic People: Their Origin, Expansion and Culture.* New Haven, 1966.
Sherk, R. K. *The Roman Empire, Augustus to Hadrian.* Cambridge, 1993.
Thompson, E. A. *The Visigoths in the Time of Ulfila.* Oxford, 1966.

**The Culture of the Germanic Empires**
Dunbabin, J. *France in the Making.* Oxford, 1985.
Goffart, W. *The Narrators of Barbarian History.* Princeton, 1989.
Herrin, J. *The Formation of Christendom.* Princeton, 1988.
Jarrett, M. G., and Dobson, B. *Britain and Rome.* Kendal, 1965.
Nelson, J. L. *Politics and Ritual in Early Medieval Europe.* London, 1986.
Philip, R. *Britain: A Granary for Rome?* Amsterdam, 1982.
Reuter, T. *Germany in the Early Middle Ages.* London, 1991.
Wallace-Hadrill, J. M. *Early Medieval History.* Oxford, 1976.

**Constantinople**
Barth, H. *Constantinople.* Paris, 1953.
Byron, R. *The Byzantine Achievement: A Historical Perspective, AD 330–1453.* New York, 1964.
Clogan, P. M. *Byzantine and Western Studies.* Totowa, 1984.
Dalton, O. *Byzantine Art and Archaeology.* Oxford, 1961.

Downey, G. *Constantinople in the Age of Justinian.* Norman, 1968.
Herrin, J. *Constantinople in the Early Eighth Century.* Leiden, 1984.
Rice, D. *Byzantine Art.* Harmondsworth, 1968.
Sherard, P. *Constantinople: Iconography of a Sacred City.* London, 1965.

**The Rule of Justinian**
Barker, J. W. *Justinian and the Later Roman Empire.* Madison, 1966.
Birks, P. *Justinian's Institutes.* New York, 1987.
Browning, R. *Justinian and Theodora.* London, 1971.
Bridge, A. *Theodora.* München, 1980.
Kolbert, C. F. *Justinian: The Digest of Roman Law.* Harmondsworth, 1979.
Moorhead, J. *Theoderic in Italy.* Oxford, 1992.
——. *Justinian.* London, 1994.
Ure, P. N. *Justinian and His Age.* Greenwood, 1979.

**The New Persian Empire**
Benveniste, E. *Persian Religion According to the Chief Greek Texts.* Paris, 1959.
Colledge, M. *The Parthians.* London, 1967.
——. *The Parthian Period.* Leiden, 1986.
Cook, J. M. *The Persian Empire.* London, 1983.
Matheson, S. A. *Persia: An Archaeological Guide.* London, 1979.
Ort, L. J. R. *Mani: A Religio-Historical Description of His Personality.* Leiden, 1967.
Ross, E. D. *Persian Art.* London, 1938.
Widengren, G. *Mani and Manichaeism.* London, 1965.

**Muhammad**
Hodges, R. *Mohammed, Charlemagne and the Origins of Europe.* New York, 1983.
Rodinson, M. *Mohammed.* Brussels, 1982.

**Islam**
Azzam, S. *Islam and Contemporary Society.* London , 1982.
Hitti, P. K. *Islam: A Way of Life.* Minneapolis, 1971.
Kateregga, B. D. *Islam and Christianity: A Muslim and a Christian in Dialogue.* Nairobi, 1985.
Martin, R. A. *Islam: A Cultural Perspective.* Englewood Cliffs, 1982.
Peters, R. *Islam and Colonialism: The Doctrine of Jihad in Modern History.* The Hague, 1979.
Rahman, F. *Islam: The History of a Religion.* London, 1966.
Roberts, D. S. *Islam: A Westerner's Guide.* London, 1981.
——. *Islam: A Concise Introduction.* San Francisco, 1982.
Sjadzali, M. *Islam and Governmental Systems: Teachings, History and Reflections.* Jakarta, 1991.
Williams, J. A. *Islam.* New York, 1967.

**Jihad**

Cudsi, A. S. *Islam and Power*. London, 1982.

Dekmejian, R. H. *Islam in Revolution: Fundamentalism in the Arab World*. New York, 1985.

Von Grunebaum, G. E. *Islam: Essays on the Nature and Growth of a Cultural Tradition*. London, 1969.

——. *Islam and Medieval Hellenism: Social and Cultural Perspectives*. London, 1976.

Lewis, B. *Islam in History: Ideas, Men and Events in the Middle East*. La Salla, 1973.

——. *Islam: From the Prophet Muhammad to the Capture of Constantinople*. London, 1976.

Makdisi, G. *Islam and the West in the Middle Ages*. Paris, 1977.

Semaan, K. I. *Islam and the Medieval West: Aspects of Intercultural Relations*. New York, 1980.

Verhoeven, F. R. J. *Islam: Its Origin and Spread in Words, Maps and Pictures*. Amsterdam, 1962.

Vryonis, S. *Islam and Cultural Change in the Middle Ages*. Wiesbaden, 1975.

**The Caliphs**

Ashtiany, J. *Abbasid Belles-lettres*. Cambridge, 1990.

Bosworth, C. E. *The Islamic Dynasties*. Edinburgh, 1980.

Frye, R. N. *Islamic Iran and Central Asia, 7th – 12th Centuries*. London, 1979.

Knappert, J. *Islamic Legend: Histories of the Heroes, Saints and Prophets of Islam*. Leiden, 1985.

Lewis, A. R. *The Islamic World and the West, AD 622–1492*. New York, 1970.

al-Qulanisi, Ibn. *The Damascus Chronicle of the Crusades*. New York, 1980.

Seddiqui, A. H. *Caliphate and Kingship in Medieval Persia*. Philadelphia, 1977.

Shaban, M. A. *The Abbasid Revolution*. Cambridge, 1979.

Sykes, M. *The Caliphs' Last Heritage*. New York, 1973.

Walker, A. T. *The Caliphate*. Oxford, 1924.

**The Riches of Islam**

Atl, E. *Islamic Art and Patronage: Treasures from Kuwait*. New York, 1990.

Brandenburg, D. *Islamic Miniature Painting in Medieval Manuscripts*. Basle, 1982.

Brend, B. *Islamic Art*. Cambridge, MA, 1991.

Burns, R. I. *Islam under the Crusaders*. Princeton, 1973.

Ettinghausen, R. *Islamic Art and Archaeology*. Berlin, 1984.

Glick, T. F. *Islamic and Christian Spain in the Early Middle Ages*. Princeton, 1979.

King, D. A. *Islamic Astronomical Instruments*. London, 1987.

Kuhnel, I. *Islamic Art and Architecture*. London, 1966.

Schimmel, A. *Islamic Calligraphy*. Leiden, 1970.

Spuhler, F. *Islamic Carpets and Textiles*. London, 1978.

# Further Reading

Alladin, B. *Story of Mohammed the Prophet*. Pomona, CA, 1979.

Aries, P. et al, eds. *A History of Private Life: From Pagan Rome to Byzantium*. Vol. 1. Cambridge, MA, 1992.

Bakhtiar, L. *History of Islam*. Chicago, 1993.

Benjamin, S. G. *The Story of Persia*. New York, 1977.

Booty, J. E. *The Church in History*. San Francisco, 1984.

Cootes, R. J. *Middle Ages*. White Plains, NY, 1989.

Curtis, J. *Ancient Persia*. Cambridge, MA, 1990.

Downey, G. *Constantinople in the Age of Justinian*. New York, 1991.

Finegan, J. *Light from the Ancient Past*. (2 vols.) Princeton, 1959.

Gordon, M. S. *Islam*. New York, 1991.

Heather, P. J. *Goths and Romans AD 332–489*. New York, 1994.

King, A. *Roman Gaul and Germany*. Berkeley, 1990.

Kohlrausch, F. *A History of Germany from the Earliest Period to the Present Time*. Saint Clair Shores, MI, 1972.

Newark, T. *The Barbarians: Warriors and Wars of the Dark Ages*. New York, 1988.

Runciman, S. *The Fall of Constantinople, 1453*. New York, 1990.

Steffens, B. *The Fall of the Roman Empire: Opposing Viewpoints*. San Diego, 1994.

Todd, M. *The Early Germans*. Cambridge, MA, 1995.

Walker, B. G. *History of the Christian Church*. New York, 1984.

Wolfram, H. *History of the Goths*. Berkeley, 1988.

# Illustration Credits

# Index

Text is indicated in roman type; illustrations are indicated in italic type.

1147

Text is indicated in roman type; illustrations are indicated in italic type.

Text is indicated in roman type; illustrations are indicated in italic type.

Text is indicated in roman type; illustrations are indicated in italic type.